DIRTY SHIRT

a boundary waters memoir

DIRTY SHIRT

a boundary waters memoir

JIM LANDWEHR

eLectio Publishing
Little Elm, TX

A portion of this book was previously published in the Winter Issue
of *Boundary Waters Journal* magazine.

In memory of my brother Rob,
a vested partner in many of these adventures.

CONTENTS

ACKNOWLEDGEMENTS   VII

PROLOGUE   IX

Part I: Friends

BOUNDARY WATERS DREAMIN'   1

RAILS, ROADS, AND REALITY   9

SETTING OUT   13

A RAPID DECLINE   19

PARTING OUR WAYS   25

THE FIX-IT TRIP   33

PLYMOUTH ROCK   37

LOST WITH THE BOSS   39

MAKING UP TIME   43

GETTING IN A RHYTHM   47

FINISHING WHAT WE STARTED   51

HITCHIN' A RIDE   53

Part II: Brothers

THE PLANNING   59

THE PACKING   65

THE DRIVING   73

THE RESTING   89

THE LAUNCHING   95

THE PADDLING   103

THE PORTAGING   117

THE FISHING   125
THE CAMPING   135
THE CLEANING   145
THE LEAVING   149

Part III: Children

OUR RETURN – 2009   161
TWO PLANS ARE BETTER THAN ONE   165
ADVENTURE 101   169
DÉJÀ VIEW   171
WEATHERING THE STORM   175
WALLEYE CHOPPED   177
LOONACY   179
ANCHORED AWAY   183
FOREST FACILITIES   185
DISASTER AVERTED   189
FISHING ECONOMICS   193
BOYS BEING BOYS   197
FISHING FOR ANSWERS   203
OUR RETURN – 2012   213
DAY 1 – MAYFLIES   217
DAY 2 – DRAGONFLIES   223
DAY 3 – WHITE MOSQUITOES FROM HELL   227
DAY 4 – MOSQUITOES   235
EPILOGUE   241

Acknowledgements

The genesis of this book was a writing workshop I took part in over nine years ago. What was intended to be nothing more than a ten-page theme has evolved over the past four years into this full-length memoir. I am forever indebted to the instructor of that workshop, Ms. Shannon Jackson Arnold. She was the one who first challenged me to take my writing seriously and sparked me into action.

If Shannon was the spark, I would have to credit Kathie Giorgio, director of AllWriters' Workplace and Workshop, with being the fuel. She has been with me throughout the process, simultaneously being my biggest fan and biggest critic. She always encouraged me when I was down or not sure where I was going with the whole project. I can't mention her without mentioning her husband, Michael, who was there as well, relentless in correcting my sentence structure and punctuation. These two, along with many of the AllWriters' students, have encouraged me to grow in the craft and legitimize my writing.

To my wife, Donna, I say thank you for your support and for giving up our Wednesday and Thursday nights together so I could go and be cerebral with my writing cronies. I love that our written words brought us together for this beautiful life we have created. My brothers Tom, Rob, and Paul and our various friends from trips past deserve mention for allowing me to write these personal memories we share—memories I deem too important to be lost when we're all gone. I extend my thanks to them for their fact checking and words of encouragement.

Finally I want to thank the staff at eLectio Publishing for believing in me and giving me a chance. You have made a lifelong dream come true, and I thank you for that.

Prologue

It's 1976 and I am fifteen, sitting cross-legged in a vintage canvas tent from the '60s with Timmy, the son of Jack, the man my mother is dating. There is an orphan tent pole dangling from the center of the ceiling, victim of either its missing base or some inferior tent assembly; no one is quite sure which. The pole's umbrella arms reach out and hold up the four tent corners, but something doesn't seem quite right. The supporting pole just hangs there in the middle of the tent looking like a Christo sculpture gone awry. The running joke around camp is about whether it really should be on the outside of the tent rather than the inside. Again, no one is quite sure.

Inside the spacious, damp tent, we are careful not to touch the sides, as we were told it causes the rain to penetrate the canvas at the touch point. The tent smells of basement and must, but it is a warm, dry refuge for us. Using a big flashlight as our source of light, Timmy is sitting across from me, teaching me how to play cribbage. The cards and game board, stuck with its scoring pegs, sit between us on the floor atop the unrolled sleeping bags. Timmy is an accomplished cardplayer for a seventeen-year-old and is patient with teaching the nuances of fifteen two, fifteen four. Santana's "Evil Ways" is playing on the black Sanyo cassette player on the tent floor. The player is the top-loading kind, meant more for taping an interview than listening to music. It certainly is not doing justice to the brilliance of Carlos Santana's guitar work as we sit here in the dark woods of northern Minnesota.

"We need Mother Nature to change *her* evil ways," Timmy says, commenting about the incessant rainy and cloudy weather we've had since our arrival.

"You got that right," I agree. The rain has ceased, at least for the moment, and my mother and Jack are outside around the pathetic, wet-wood smolder they call a campfire. Timmy and I, bored with trying to coax the smoking mass to life, have sought refuge in our tent and have left the fire to our respective parents. If the weather pattern continues as it has, it's only a matter of time before the drops will begin to fall and drive our parents into the tent, as well. For now, they're trying to make the best of the respite from the bad weather while enjoying a camper's nightcap.

"Ooooo, what's that thing?" Timmy asks, pointing to a greyish worm-like thing on the floor of the tent, near one of the corners.

"Yuck! I don't know; I think it's a slug or something," I reply.

"Whatever it is, it's nasty. What if it crawls on us while we're sleeping?"

"Thanks for bringing up that possibility!" I say. Timmy flicks the slug back down into the hole in the corner of the tent from which it came.

"Look, there's another one," Timmy says as he points to the wall of the tent, where one is hanging. "They're everywhere," he exaggerates. I join him in his expressions of disgust at the slimy, albeit harmless, creatures that have taken up residence in our tent. Like us, they are probably just looking for someplace dry after the deluge of the previous day. While I am certain there has never been a case of death by slug, I am also sure, thanks to Timmy, that I will be sleeping lightly on this damp night.

We are at a small campground on Iron Lake, on the edge of, but not *in*, the Boundary Waters Canoe Area of northern Minnesota. I struggle with the dichotomy that we have come to this godforsaken place of our own accord and that, at the same time, there is something mystically attractive about it. I am here with my brother Tom, my mother, Jack, and Jack's two sons, Patrick and Timmy. Mom and Jack have been dating for seven years, so my five siblings and I have become friends with many of his eight kids. Tom, twenty-one, befriended Patrick, who is the same age. Timmy is two years older than me, but we attend the same high school and have become friends as well. This trip was suggested by Mom and Jack as an "older boys" trip up to the Gunflint Trail for what they referred to as some "real camping." My older sisters, Pat and Jane, are back home taking care of my younger brothers, Rob and Paul.

Our campsite at the moment is clearly more remote and rugged than I've ever seen. When they said we were going "real camping," they were not kidding. The rutted gravel roads we took to get here, the thick tree canopy, and smelly pit toilets are all testament to that. We've camped several times before in much less remote areas closer to our home in the Twin Cities. Those trips usually involved a mix of kids from both families, two monstrous tents, and a couple of large sedans with trunks and rooftops loaded with equipment.

My mom and Jack are firm believers that tent camping is the only true camping and that trailers and RVs are for the weak and infirm. This trip to the edge of nothingness is a manifestation of their belief, and while I profess to be among the brethren of the rugged-camping enlightened, I have moments where my faith is tested. While the slugs and incessant rain are not cause enough for me to change over my allegiance to the RV heathen, when coupled with all the other annoyances of the trip, I believe I am having my biblical Job moment.

* * *

It is the next morning and, for however briefly, the sun has chosen to shine on our camp. Mom heats some water on the dual-burner Coleman stove to clean up the breakfast dishes, while Timmy and I pick up around camp and get ready for a day of canoeing on Iron Lake. Tom and Patrick are over in their own campsite adjacent to us, "goofing off." Last night Patrick climbed a small, very dead tree until his weight forced it to the tipping point, when he let out a Tarzan scream and braced himself for landing. This was followed by much guffawing. When Mom asks them about their escapades this morning, they laugh guiltily and claim they were doing it in the name of gathering firewood. I give them credit for originality.

When breakfast is finished, we drive to the Gunflint Lodge outfitter to rent the canoes we will be using. The Gunflint Trail is a winding two-lane highway, and its many curves and bends turn a nine-mile trip into a twenty-minute ride. We arrive and spend a few minutes stretching our legs and admiring the beauty of Gunflint Lake before we pay for the rental canoes and load them onto the cars. While we are driving away from the lodge, the skies open up again and it starts to pour. The rain comes down so hard we have to pull the cars over momentarily and wait for it to slow down. As the rain pounds on the canoe over the car's roof, I think about what it must be like back in the tent at camp. I suspect it's dry, but I'm glad I'm in a vehicle at the moment. It becomes apparent that this is not just another camping trip. The remoteness of the area and the weather's wet fury have served to ratchet the adventure quotient up a notch.

Eventually the rain stops and we are granted a brief reprieve as we drive to the boat launch at Iron Lake. Tom and Patrick unload their canoe at the water's edge, while Jack and Timmy muscle the second one alongside it. Mom and I help with life jackets, paddles, and personal items. Mom climbs into the bow and I sit on a cushion on the floor of the long aluminum canoe. Jack steps into the stern and pushes us off into the lake. When we are stable and paddling, Jack lights a cigarette and then tucks the pack back into a Ziploc bag to keep them dry.

I am immediately aware of the serenity and the quiet. Though motors are allowed on the lake, there are none this day. There are no lodges or cabins or docks. It is calm and pristine; we can hear nothing but the wind in the trees, our voices, and the occasional bump of the paddles against the sides of the canoe. Much of the shoreline is comprised of large lichen-covered rock outcrops jutting skyward that make for majestic vistas as we round each bend. An eagle soars overhead. Having never seen an eagle in the wild, I am enthralled by both the grace of its flight and the transcendent natural experience.

We come to a large rocky cliff shooting twenty feet out of the water. The rock wall has a ledge about halfway up. It looks to be accessible by way of a short steep trail and some nifty rock-climbing skills. Patrick, Timmy, and Jack are all accomplished swimmers and see it as an opportunity for a nice cliff dive. Tom drops off Patrick and Timmy on the shore, while Mom and I do the same with Jack. Someone has to stay behind and watch the canoes, so the three weakest swimmers kindly volunteer. The three divers climb the cliff with sure caution and stand at the top, assessing their strategy for the big jump.

All at once, Patrick notices a coiled-up snake sleeping on the cliff. He tells us it's only a harmless garter snake, but Jack doesn't care. He's afraid of all snakes, regardless of their size. It is the perfect incentive for him to be first to get off the cliff. He springs out with a diver's form and splashes into the cool water. The sadistic side of Patrick comes out and he decides to prey on his father's snake phobia. He grabs the snake and throws it into the water near Jack.

Jack screams a guttural man-scream and starts swimming away at top speed. He is a former navy man and an excellent swimmer, which works to his advantage here. The snake isn't interested in a water attack and is likely more frightened about the encounter than Jack is. It zigzags toward shore and is soon out of sight. Mom and I paddle to an area nearby and hold the canoe steady while Jack climbs back in.

Patrick and Timmy dive in one after the other, each with a different degree of grace and form. The two of them swim back to their canoe and manage to flop back in. As a group, we continue on our paddle, exploring the lake and enjoying the area and the pleasant change in the weather.

The rest of the trip is filled with wonderful firsts for me—everything from picking wild raspberries to hauling over the rollercoaster-like dirt roads at perilous speeds in Mom's Impala with Tom at the wheel to eating Hamburger Helper inside the tent because of a sudden downpour. It is a spectacular adventure for me at that age, and my appetite is whetted for more.

* * *

That trip, with all of its calamities and wonder, was the catalyst for future visits with friends and family that would become the source of many great memories for me. These trips took me further north, deeper into the woods under even more rustic conditions. The area drew me in and I sought adventure, fishing, and raw outdoor experiences. Iron Lake was a tune-up, setting the stage for future outings that I was determined to take to the next level. I look back at the trip as a gift given me by my mom and Jack—one I hope to pass on to my own kids, given the chance.

What follows is an account of my experiences in the rugged wilderness known as the Boundary Waters Canoe Area. It's sort of a CliffsNotes version of the dramas played out over a period of many years. I was somewhat hesitant to pen these thoughts for a couple of reasons.

First and foremost is my concern for preserving the character and integrity of the people involved. My attempts at humorous inflection on the events contained herein are testimony to the characters' abilities to laugh at themselves, when needed, and at others when appropriate. A solid sense of humor is essential to the whole camping experience. Love of the outdoors and the inevitable laughter that comes along with it fuels my spirit. The characters in the stories are real, loving people who helped shape me into the person I am today. To laugh *with* them requires, at times, laughing *at* them and being laughed at myself. None of it is intended to demean or insult.

The second reason I had reservations about trying to recall the events of twenty years ago is my belief that there is something to be said for the sanctity of stories shared between a few people, especially family. In some situations, oral tradition is what works best and should serve as the mechanism by which a memory or situation is relived. My peace comes from knowing there are numerous untold tales that will continue to function as the mortar between the brick foundation of our brotherhood and friendships.

Regardless, I feel compelled to share these stories, not only for my family and friends but for future generations as well. I cherish the stories of my father's life that have been passed down to me by my mother and extended family. This book is my attempt to give substance to some of my past for my own children. At the same time, it is written with hope that it might spur you, your family, and your friends to appreciate the beauty, the wonder, and the experience that can only be had in the Boundary Waters.

Part I: Friends

Part 1: Friends

Boundary Waters Dreamin'

Our trip to the Boundary Waters Canoe Area (BWCA) of northern Minnesota was, truthfully, a considerable downgrade for the four of us high school friends. The original plan was to drive west to California after graduation. When you're eighteen, you take your newly ordained adulthood as a chance to assert your independence. What better way to do that than to drive two thousand miles with your friends? Since none of us owned a car or had the money or means to get much further west than South Dakota, we "right-sized" our dreams into a five-day canoe trip. The *California Dreamin'* was good while it lasted.

The BWCA is a million-plus acres of relatively untouched wilderness extending from northern Minnesota to the Canadian border. It consists of more than a thousand lakes strung together by crystal-clear rivers and man-made portages cut through the dense forest. No motorized vehicles are allowed into the area, so all travel must be done on foot or in canoes. The natural beauty, abundant wildlife, and deafening quiet of the deep wilderness make the area attractive to any outdoor purist.

Disregard the fact that after five days in this natural beauty, I wanted nothing more than to leave it—leave it and seek such niceties as running water, hot showers, and the female form. Being in the woods, while good for the soul, is hard on the body. There's something about wilderness living that assures me the Industrial Revolution was a good thing.

There were four of us high school buddies altogether—Pete, Doug, me, and Pat, whom I still consider a best friend today. We did most of our organizing at a planning meeting in the basement of Pat's house. Doug brought a map and we planned the route, charted paddling distances, and set schedules—all things that seemed like rational, logical thoughts at the time. However, we were oblivious to the fact that, in the BWCA, the schedule is always the *first* thing to go. As wilderness rookies, we had to give the appearance of actually having a plan by charting out where we would eat, sleep, and fish. In reality, by the time we set up our tent on the first night, we were already behind schedule. We quickly realized that the only time that matters in the woods is how long until dark. For the most part, when it gets dark, everything stops.

Because most of us were eighteen and were relying entirely on our own means for transportation, there was relatively little parental input into the planning process. My guess is they were just relieved that we shed the California trip for something more local and attainable. The travel plan we crafted using our collective teenage brain trust was to start out by train from St. Paul to Duluth, Minnesota. From there we would catch the Greyhound bus to Grand Marais, a hundred miles northeast. We would then rely on hitchhiking sixty miles up the Gunflint Trail to the outfitters at our "starting point." Sounds like a slam dunk, doesn't it? Yes sir, no possible holes in that itinerary. Rock solid.

*   *   *

Much of what makes or breaks a camping trip is the quality and selection of equipment. This was our first foray into the woods without parents or other family involved. We packed what we thought would work best given our experience and substandard budget. None of us knew any better or had the means to do anything about it if we did. Besides, it was just a canoe trip; how hard could it be? We would quickly learn how unforgiving the water and woods were to ungainly equipment and poor planning.

During the planning meeting, the subject of tents was brought up.

"I've got a couple of two-man tents. One is brand new and the other is pretty beat. I think the zipper may even be broken. It's down in my basement somewhere. You're welcome to use it, but there are no guarantees on it," I said.

After a few shrugs, no one else offered anything better, so we decided to make it work. When you're a pie-eyed high school grad, you can make anything work. Needless to say, I was happy I made the investment in the new Eureka a few weeks before. My brother Tom always said that you cannot underestimate the value of a good tent, and I certainly knew which tent of the two I was sleeping in.

The rest of the equipment we took with us bordered on substandard and was designed more for car-camping than canoeing and portaging. Of course there was the "essential" Coleman lantern that would provide light for playing cards, warding off black bears, sending SOS signals to aircraft overhead, and the like. It sounded good on paper; unfortunately, we neglected to factor in the possibility of broken mantles. Mantles are small sacks or pouches made of cloth. They tie to the gas outlets on a lantern and when they burn they turn to ash, serving as the ignition point for the lantern. They work fine as long as the ashen mantles are not bumped or broken. If they are broken, what you have on your hands amounts to a low-grade civilian flamethrower. They can be fun if you're sporting an asbestos flannel shirt and a welder's helmet, but otherwise, they're pretty useless in the woods.

After discovering the broken mantles, there were many moments when heaving the useless device into the woods seemed like the most prudent thing to do—a kind of a deep-woods Molotov cocktail for the city boys. Instead, the item became our boat anchor. Not in the literal sense, but rather it was the item which, when rendered inoperable, suddenly became dead weight that had to be lugged around for the duration of the trip. Every trip has one.

Another poorly chosen article for a couple of us on the trip was the cumbersome, large cotton-filled sleeping bags. Why mess with goose down when you could lug what amounted to a seven-pound cotton sponge on your back? They were bulky and heavy when dry; when wet, they quickly doubled in weight. Ounce for ounce, they were undoubtedly the most burdensome items on the trip.

Perhaps the most definitive of all bad equipment choices was the folding drab-green military shovel. Unlike the cotton "sleeping bag sponges" and the "lantern flambeau," which had functional purposes behind being packed, this item's utility escapes me even to this day. Lord, what were we thinking? It turns out foxholes aren't really necessary on most campouts. Trenches not so much, either. If a US-Canadian war were to break out, though, we were set.

Some good advice for any camping trip is if you can't eat it, wear it, sleep in it, or start a fire with it, leave it home.

Once the equipment was defined, we focused on choosing our route. We used a popular map series that existed for the area at the time. Having spent my entire career in computer mapping, I can appreciate many of the good qualities of these maps. They were simple to read, had decent cartography, and, for the most part, had credible content. They also had a light film coating that gave them a crackly feel and made them water resistant. This worked to our advantage when water from the canoe paddles would drip on them during our paddling. I can also attest that they float for short periods of time if blown overboard, but that is another story.

For all of the good qualities these maps have, I also recognize their shortcomings: small issues such as missing or incorrect portages, scale problems, and of course, the question of how up-to-date they are. To the manufacturer's credit, however, they do have one of the most all-encompassing disclaimers I've ever seen, which reads:

This map is not intended for navigational use and is not represented to be correct in every respect.

Wow. A map not intended for navigation. My question then becomes, what is it supposed to be used for? Birdcage lining? Fish wrap? Fire kindling? Now, kindling was an idea we gave some thought to.

It's a bit like publishing a cookbook and then disclaiming it by saying, "Hey, this book shouldn't be used to cook anything." Or perhaps it's like the weatherman saying there's a forty percent chance of rain. What does that really mean? The map might serve people better by taking a meteorological approach and saying, "You have a forty percent chance of getting lost if you use this map." At least give me some odds to work with.

We continued our planning despite the heavily disclaimed map. Using it, we plotted a circuitous route that began at the outfitters on Seagull Lake, who would drop us off at our entry point on Gunflint Lake. From there we would head north, then west, and then back south, eventually finishing at the outfitters back on Seagull Lake. The map indicated several portages that circumvented fast or impassible water using a dashed line. We knew portaging was part of the whole experience, so it did not deter us from sticking with the plan. In fact, the possibility of a little excitement was alluring to all of us. The entire route would be an ambitious yet achievable paddle, especially for four young men in good physical condition.

The final planning details centered on meals and the food we would bring. It was unanimous that trying to make a meal plan comprised of freeze-dried food would be prohibitively expensive. I pointed out that as long as we brought dried food and no meat, we would probably be okay.

"Oh, we can bring meat. My brother has brought hamburger up before," Doug chimed in.

"How does he keep it from spoiling?" I asked.

"You just freeze it real good and pack it in ice. No problem."

I looked at him with questioning cynicism. My brother Tom, who had been to the area on a few occasions and whom I deemed the expert, always said that food requiring ice would add more bulk and weight than lugging it around would be worth. Furthermore, if you choose to bring frozen food, you should use dry ice as it lasts longer and does not melt. I am not sure if I mentioned the idea of dry ice, but I am sure my skepticism about bringing meat shone through fairly implicitly. Doug seemed sure and confident, so we agreed he would pack it and we would have hamburgers for a couple of our dinners. With the last of the details planned, we said our goodbyes and left, anxious and excited for our coming adventure.

*   *   *

While the planning was done corporately, we were all in charge of packing our own clothes, sleeping bags, and other equipment. I started by setting up and airing out the two tents in the front yard. The new Eureka was set up in less than ten minutes and was a thing of strength and beauty. Its poles stretched the cream-colored nylon rainfly taut, and the zippered screening was solid defense against mosquitoes and other bugs. I would go so far as to say the inside had that new tent smell, not unlike the smell of a new car.

The second tent took a bit more setup. The poles and joints were not as nicely engineered as the Eureka and it quickly became clear it was a cheap knockoff model. Unlike the Eureka with its subtle cream color, its homely brother was highway-cone orange and visible from a mile away. The only subtle quality about it was the protection it would provide against the bugs, considering its broken zipper. It was more of the Charlie Brown variety, difficult to assemble and almost as difficult to look at.

As the evening grew late, I moved on to packing my clothes. I stuffed a couple of shirts, pants, underwear, and socks into the hand-me-down frame backpack I inherited when Tom upgraded. When I went to pack what was probably my most essential piece of clothing, my heavy-duty flannel shirt, I realized it was dirty.

I mentioned to my brother Tom that my favorite camping shirt was in the laundry and it was too late to try to wash it.

Now, he had been watching most of the packing process with great amusement, sprinkled with moments of disbelief, and felt compelled to offer some sage words of wisdom.

"You know, Jim, it's always good to start a trip with a dirty shirt."

His tone was dripping with sarcasm. It became the haunting voice of reason in my head for the rest of the trip. The actual dirty shirt was the least of my issues. It was the basic precepts behind starting a trip of such magnitude with substandard equipment and planning that haunted us in so many situations. The thing was, I knew he was right. Tom was a seasoned camper who backpacked his way across the country a few years earlier. I was determined to do this trip *my way*, however. I wanted to prove I could do it as well as anyone, so I chose to press on and make my indelible mark in the woods.

The scars are still healing.

Rails, Roads, and Reality

On the day we were to leave, we met at the Amtrak station in St. Paul. Ahead of us lay a three-hour train ride up to Duluth. We checked our packs and found four seats near each other. Traveling by train was relaxing, and we filled the time reading, joking, gazing out the window, and napping. There was an air of excitement with what we were about to undertake. We were free from the bonds of high school and home life, and we were ready to expend some young energy.

We arrived in Duluth in the late morning, anxious to get on the bus to Grand Marais. When we found the Greyhound station, we discovered we would have a three-hour wait until the next bus left. With each of us tethered to a fifty-pound pack, there was a limit to what we could do to pass the time. We did what typical teens of the time would do. We hung out in the local laundromat and drank soda. It was a hot day, and that seemed like a prudent thing to do.

Because of the heat and the fact that we had so much time to kill, Doug decided he should check on the ground beef he packed in Tupperware with ice cubes. It turns out the ice was completely melted and had leaked all over his backpack as well. I caught Pat's eye and we shared a look of grave incredulity. It should have served as a bellwether warning for the rest of the trip. While it was nice to be validated that my argument against bringing meat was correct, at the same time, the main course for our dinner for the first two nights was now floating in cool water. There are only two words that can describe our meal prognosis at that point: not good.

"That doesn't look promising," Pat said.

"No, it doesn't. But it will be alright if we eat it tonight and tomorrow night," Doug replied.

We all agreed that was a decent plan of action for a seemingly declining situation. We tried not to let it dampen our spirits. After all, we were on vacation and were more than a hundred miles from our parents. We were free! No need for a minor setback like this to get us down. Double cheeseburgers tonight, all around!

The Greyhound arrived on schedule and we were happy to hop on board and get moving again. It was a long but enjoyable ninety-minute drive up the scenic north shore of Lake Superior, inasmuch as any ride on a bus can be enjoyable.

By midafternoon, the bus came to a stop and its parking brake hissed our arrival in downtown Grand Marais, a town of about a thousand people. We shook out the cramps from our ride and started walking toward the Gunflint Trail. The trail is a sixty-mile highway that winds and curves through stretches of forest spattered with a multitude of clean, iron-rich lakes. Because its destination ultimately serves to land people in the middle of nowhere, it is not a highly traveled route. Knowing this, we were banking on the fellowship and courtesy that campers tend to show toward other campers, especially those on foot, thumbing a ride. We had hopes and expectations that others would more correctly call delusions.

To better our odds of catching a ride, we split up; Pete and I were together, and Doug and Pat were the second pair. We stayed close enough to ensure that oncoming cars would see us and make the connection that we were all together yet still willing to separate if someone only had room for two. If that happened, we agreed we would eventually catch up with each other at the end of the trail.

We began walking up the highway shoulder. Our legs were fresh and, though the packs were heavy, we knew we were one short car ride from our destination. A car approached and the four of us turned around, stuck out our thumbs, and tried to beg a ride. The car, loaded with passengers, equipment, and a canoe, sped by without so much as slowing. We all had hitchhiked enough to know the game was one of numbers, never in favor of the hiker, so we turned around and kept walking.

As we walked, our heads were shrouded with bugs. We used bug spray, but it had little effect. It was early June and mosquito, gnat, and horsefly season was near its zenith. The mosquitoes weren't as bad if we were moving, but when we stopped, we went from being men to being a food source. Gnats that once just annoyed now landed and bit. Some took the kamikaze approach into our ears and eyes. Stopping also enabled the mosquitoes to catch up, and when they did, they were in drill-and-kill mode.

The bloodthirsty insects actually motivated us to keep moving forward. By walking we were at least making progress, albeit glacially slow. It certainly beat standing there doing the bug dance with arms and legs flailing in pinwheel fashion. So we walked, and walked, and thumbed, and fanned gnats, and walked some more.

After some time, Pete and I separated far enough ahead of Doug and Pat that we could no longer see them. It was nearing dusk, we had been hitchhiking all afternoon, and we were still yet to catch a ride. The two of us came to an unpaved road with a sign referencing a nearby Boy Scout camp.

Pete looked at me. "You thinkin' what I'm thinkin'?"

"I sure am. Let's stay here for tonight."

"Hopefully Pat and Doug aren't too far behind and will see our tent."

We dropped our packs and set up camp in a clearing a short distance from the highway. We wanted to be sure Pat and Doug could see us if they should still be on foot and happen by. Within a half hour, we heard them talking as they came up the road. They saw the tent and joined us in our hobo camp.

"Tough goin', huh?" Pat asked.

"Yep, sure was," Pete answered.

"Nice place you've got here," Pat said with a laugh.

He and Doug found a clearing across the path from us, set up their secondhand tent, and rolled out their sleeping bags. When they were finished, we talked about what we should have for dinner. Because we were not in an authorized campsite, we all agreed we should probably not have a fire. Instead we opted for trail mix, cheese, and a couple Slim Jims. Darkness was closing in fast and the mosquitoes were working up to a full frenzy. Tired after our long day of travel, we all decided to escape the bugs in the safety of our tents immediately after dinner. Tomorrow would be a better day.

Or so we thought.

Setting Out

As we crawled out of our tents the following morning, I caught a bit of wrath for suggesting we bring a tent with a faulty zipper. Pat and Doug spent much of the night staving off mosquito attacks and trying to devise ways to make a tighter seal on the gapped screen door of the tent. I reminded everyone that the tent provision came with a well-defined disclaimer. After a quick breakfast of Pop-Tarts, we packed up and headed back out to the highway.

Our collective luck was significantly better on day two, at least regarding our land travel. Shortly after we started hitchhiking, all four of us landed a ride in the back of a pickup truck. We threw our packs in and climbed aboard. The bed of the truck was hard and the ride was bumpy and highly illegal, but I was happy to be moving forward under something other than my own power. Our luck continued when we told the driver where we were headed and he nodded that he could take us all the way to our destination at Seagull Outfitters.

After thanking the driver, we filed into the outfitters. The wide-open log cabin smelled of leather and wood smoke. Equipment and packs were hanging from pegs behind the long, varnished pine counter. Maps, brochures, and candy bars were set out to entice impulsive shoppers. An occasional mosquito buzzed in and out of view, a reminder of what we went through the day before.

"What can I do for you guys?" the proprietor asked.

"We're looking to rent a couple of canoes," Doug said.

"Sure thing. Where is your departure point?"

He pulled out some maps and we explained our intended route. As we went over our course with the outfitter, he pointed out areas where we could probably "shoot" the whitewater and stretches that would be best avoided. We took advantage of his advice, marking our copy of the map per his recommendations. When he asked about our experience, he seemed a bit skeptical about our collective skill set. Given his investment of two aluminum canoes and the fact that none of us was much more than a canoeing novice, it was probably a righteous anxiety.

Before we settled up with our deposits, the outfitter picked up his phone and called someone to request a drop-off for the four of us at Gunflint Lake. Within ten minutes, the driver arrived and we piled in the big eleven-person van. It bumped along the narrow highway back down the trail about ten miles to our starting point on Gunflint Lake. When we arrived, we grabbed our packs while the van driver set to untying the canoes. We helped him lift them off and set them in the water. As we began loading our gear into the canoes, Pete noticed one of them had a nail-sized leak on the floor near the bow. The boat was taking on water at an alarming rate.

"Hey, we got a leaker here!" Pete quickly motioned to the driver behind the wheel of the van, just moments from leaving us. The man climbed out of the van and, after assessing the issue, said he'd have to run the defective canoe back to the outfitter and get a replacement. All of us were upset with the ensuing time setback, but there was little we could do about it. We were on the edge of our launch point and it would take more than a leaky canoe to get us down.

We unpacked our gear and set it on the shore. Doug grabbed one end of the second-rate boat and helped the driver load it on top of the van. In a few minutes, he was on his way. We waited around for an hour, grateful to be near water, where the bugs were tolerable. When the driver returned, we traded the leaker for the upgrade and reloaded the canoe, checking closely for leaks but finding none. We said goodbye to the van driver and shoved off into the open water. The whole ordeal set us another hour behind schedule. It wasn't a show-stopping delay, but our bad luck was beginning to seem ominous.

Following the map, we paddled a short distance and took a left turn into Magnetic Lake. Spirits were high and we were all happy to be away from the bugs and finally making progress. A half hour into our journey, as our thirst began to develop, Doug was quick to point out that the water up this far north was so clean you could drink it right out of the lake. On a couple of occasions, he dipped his cup in and drank big gulps of the untreated water. The rest of us were more skeptical and used caution, only drinking small amounts. None of us packed fresh water because our plan was to boil it for meals and hydration. Since we did not have a portable stove and were still a while from having a campfire, we had to make do with what lay before or, in this case, beneath us.

Magnetic Lake was beautiful, albeit much smaller than Gunflint. When we crossed it, we were funneled into the Pine River system. The current was swift, making our paddling easier as we began making up some lost time. In between warning each other of submerged rocks, we chatted between the two canoes, talking about music, girls, and our plans for the future after high school. All of us were accepted for enrollment at the University of Minnesota in the fall. Pete and Doug had definite ideas on what they wanted to pursue, whereas Pat and I were still unsure.

After a couple of short portages, it was approaching noon and we were all getting hungry. We decided to pull over and have some lunch. We pulled the canoes up and secured them on shore. Immediately upon stepping out of his canoe, Doug ambled off into the woods, mumbling something about not feeling so good. A couple of minutes later he rejoined us, vowing not to drink any more untreated lake water for the rest of the trip. Snickers rippled through the group as is common among men when others toss their lunch. Of course this was strange, twisted behavior given our friend's condition, but it was as close as men come to mustering up any empathy for each other. We would do anything for each other, but puking was just dang funny.

As we began rummaging through the food pack for something to fill the void, Doug decided to check on the status of the hamburger in the Tupperware. When he opened the lid, he found that the meat had turned a ghastly shade of white. All of the natural coloring had drained into the melted ice water. It didn't smell bad yet, but it was surely on the way. The meat had all the appeal of a dirty, sweaty sock floating in toilet water.

"Anyone hungry?" Doug joked.

I took a look and groaned, "Oh, man, that looks horrible!"

Pat and Pete took a peek to see what all of the hubbub was about. They reacted with the same level of disgust. Doug took the hamburger out of its plastic wrapping and heaved what amounted to two meals worth of blonde burger to the bears. At least someone would be eating well tonight.

The afternoon sun was warm as we snacked on granola and apples at the portage, replenishing calories burned from a hard morning's paddle. When we finished, we shoved off and pushed northward down the Pine River toward our next major portage at Pine Island. The river had decent depth to it, though there were still plenty of large submerged rocks lurking beneath to keep us on our toes. Many of those glistened with aluminum residue that marked the passage of prior travelers. In areas where the river narrowed, the water picked up speed and became a dangerous, raging beast.

At some point in our journey down the Pine, we took a wrong turn. When we glanced at the map, landmarks were not showing up where we expected them. We were having trouble locating the Pine Island portage and, after doubling back in confusion a couple of times, we pulled the canoes alongside each other to discuss where we were. What resulted was a lot of map rotating, locational speculation, and even a couple of wild-assed guesses. It was our first exposure to the confusing nature of extreme remote wilderness and we were learning on the fly. When all you have around you are trees and water, with no signs or buildings or roads, things all tend to look the same.

About the only thing we knew for sure was that we needed to cross two sets of rapids to get around the island and resume our originally intended route. We decided we would continue onward and scout the rapids rather than continue to look for the portage. After a minute or two, we arrived at the first set of rapids. The whitewater was not raging, but it was impressive enough to cause us to pause. It was clearly nothing we were going to try to paddle through. There did, however, appear to be a calmer-water pathway along the right bank of the river. Somehow the idea was hatched that if we rigged ropes to the canoes and essentially walked or guided them down this channel, we might save ourselves from having to unload the canoes and do the portage the hard way.

Everyone piled out of the boats and we started tying our ropes to the bows and sterns. When that was done, we each took an end and started our canoe walking. The deception of the river's powerful current became obvious very quickly. What appeared as calm water took on schizophrenia when we started playing canoe wrangler with our ropes and teenage brawn. The current quickly took control of Pat and Doug's boat and made them earn every step.

"Don't let that rear end get turned!" Doug shouted.

"Yeah, I got it," Pat said reassuringly.

They pulled and tugged, digging in with their feet when necessary, eventually imposing their will on the boat. They successfully brought the canoe to the bottom of the rapids with nothing more than shaken nerves and raw hands.

Pete and I began our descent right after Pat and Doug. We fought the same battle, at one point nearly losing the entire canoe. We played give-and-take with the river, attempting to prove our dominion over it. As we slowly worked our way forward, the canoe's stern got pulled into the current, turned, and tipped far enough to take on water over the side, soaking the bottom of the packs.

"Grab it! Grab it and pull!" Pete yelled.

"I got it, I got it!" I answered.

When I yanked the stern back into submission, the quick adjustment caused my brand-new sleeping bag to fall into the current and float downstream.

"Hey, can you grab that?" I shouted to Pat and Doug.

"Yeah, I'll get it," Pat said, and he jumped knee-deep in the river and fetched it.

"Thanks, man. I appreciate it."

Pete and I continued to tussle with the defiant canoe from the shore. After a few more tense moments, we managed to get to the bottom of the rapids and joined the other two. We unloaded the equipment and tipped the canoe to drain the water out. It was becoming apparent that our effort to save a little work was becoming a lot of work. When the canoe was emptied of water, we reloaded and climbed back in. In less than five minutes, we arrived at the second set of rapids.

A Rapid Decline

The four of us looked at the raging whitewater and assessed our chances of negotiating our sixteen-foot aluminum canoes through it without loss of equipment, life, or limb. The water churned and roiled with humbling voracity. If rated, these rapids were likely of the class-four variety or certainly a high three. The problem lay in us, the class-one paddlers who, at the age of eighteen, were clearly more confident than we had any right to be.

Being lost and tired with nightfall looming changes the game in the great wilderness. Clear thinking sometimes gives way to risky decisions or bad judgment. For us, concerns about finding a site, setting up camp, and cooking a warm meal were at the forefront of our minds. We had been traveling since daybreak on day two of our five-day trip and had taken a couple of wrong turns from our proposed route. The promise of dinner and a warm tent just on the other side of this set of menacing rapids seemed too good to pass up. Besides, we were up for a bit of excitement. To us, it seemed more like a great adventure—something you see in the movies—than an inexcusable rookie mistake-in-the-making. A wrong decision could potentially ruin a good trip or even seriously injure any of the four of us. However, the thought of lugging all our gear over the rugged portage and then repeating the trip with the canoes outweighed any sensibilities. A ten-second ride through the whitewater seemed the path of least resistance to all of us.

"I think if we stay to the right over there"—I motioned with my finger near the beginning of the rapids—"and then cut back left near that rock, we'll be okay."

The others all agreed. It seemed to be the most logical route, at least to our untrained eyes. Having made our decision, we all strapped on our life jackets and double-checked the equipment in the canoes. Doug and Pat elected to take on the rapids first. Pete and I would watch, and once they made it we would follow in our canoe.

They started into the fast current headed toward the raging waters below, Pat in the bow and Doug astern. They dug in with determination with their wooden paddles, attempting to follow the course we agreed upon. They shouted commands to each other; "Hard right, hard right! Yep, yep, there we go!" At the midpoint the boat listed enough to one side to have water come over the gunwale. They made a quick correction and, with the exception of taking on a few gallons of liquid cargo, came out the other end relatively unscathed.

"Got a little water, but it's not too bad. Just stay to the right," Doug shouted back to us.

Although it didn't look as technically difficult for Pat and Doug as we feared, Pete and I still had reservations. Neither of us was an accomplished canoeist, and I was not much of a swimmer, either. Pete literally saved my life during an incident a year earlier on the St. Croix River. He pulled me to shore when I grew exhausted by the current and told him I couldn't make it. Based on my history, I had every reason to have the jitters in these waters. About all we had going for us was a liberal dose of teen spirit and a quest for adventure.

So Pete and I set out for our moment of whitewater glory. Pete took the stern and I was tasked with scouting boulders in the bow.

"Are you ready?" Pete asked.

"Yep. Let's do this."

We plunged our paddles into the strong current and pushed off the shore. We barely began to paddle when we were wrenched sideways and pinned between two submerged rocks. The canoe rolled slightly to one side and we took on about an inch of water before we were able to right it and stop the incoming flow. We both climbed out and tried to steady the boat in the rushing current.

Pete asked me with a look of panic, "Oh, man, what do we do now?"

"I don't know. We can't really drag it backwards in this current."

"Should we go for it then?" Pete questioned.

"Yeah, I guess so."

We wrestled the canoe out from between the two rocks, and I slogged back into my spot in the front while Pete steadied the canoe. Pete climbed in and we were off again.

We dug our paddles hard into the rushing water, occasionally getting jarred when hitting a hidden submerged rock.

"Right, right!" I shouted from my perch, looking into the swirling maelstrom. We were headed for a large boulder to our left.

"I know, I know!" Pete yelled back.

The canoe lurched as it struck the boulder with great force. The back end swung around wildly in the current and before I could shout "Mayday!" we flipped into the swirling torrent. The water was shockingly cold and disorienting, as it is whenever one is dunked against their will.

As I came toward the surface, my skull thumped on the floor of the overturned boat. For a few seconds, I was trapped beneath it. Realizing my predicament, I flailed and thrashed in the cold, rushing rage. For a moment, I became panic-stricken that I wouldn't be able to get out from under it. It was the first time I'd ever seen my life flash before my eyes. This was it; I would die under the boat in the raging whitewater. As a course of death, it certainly beats wasting away in a nursing home, but at the time I preferred to postpone it a few years, if possible.

The water was deep enough that I couldn't easily touch bottom. Fortunately, the buoyant life vest brought me to the surface a second time and allowed me to get my bearings. Having been spared a watery death, I floundered and thrashed down the river, taking on the whitewater the way God intended me to.

The submerged canoe continued banging its way down the rapids sans its crew as we swam toward it at the bottom. The two of us grabbed onto it and dragged its submerged aluminum carcass to the shore. I glanced up to see my sleeping bag, for the second time in less than four hours, had managed to spring free and bobbed on the surface like an oversized polyfill cork. I yelled ahead to Pat and Doug, who were watching the synchronized drowning from the shore. They quickly maneuvered their canoe and plucked my bag out of the water, yet again.

Pete and I stood there in shock and disbelief. After we realized how lucky we were, we managed a laugh at the insanity of the whole incident. It is a bit like rolling a car and coming out without a scratch. You have to laugh at the fact that you survived, because if you don't, you'll break down and cry. After our light moment, we finished dragging the canoe to shore, emptied out the gear that survived, and then emptied out all of the water.

We took stock of the loss and damages. Somehow, our food pack and my personal backpack managed to stay in the canoe through all of the turmoil. It was all soaking wet, but at least we hadn't lost it. Thankfully, before we started down the rapids, we took measures to wedge the two packs underneath the thwarts (the bars crossing the inside of a canoe in the front and rear) and, by a stroke of luck, they held.

"Well, I lost my towel, tackle box, and fishing rod," I said.

"I don't think I lost anything, but it looks like we popped some rivets." Pete pointed to the bow deck. Four rivets were sheared off and the deck's aluminum was peeled back like a sardine can. It was nothing that would prevent us from continuing our journey, but it was certainly testament to the force of the water and rock.

"That will cost us some scratch," Pete said.

"Yeah, to add insult to injury," I replied.

The two of us wrung out our shirts, reloaded the battle-worn canoe, and set off with Pat and Doug to find a campsite for the night. It was then that the demeanor of the whole group shifted from upbeat and carefree to sober and serious. We all knew our food pack was wet and it put a damper on everything. No one knew what the next few days would hold in store, but it was clear we could not have gotten off to a worse start. We paddled for a short distance and took the first campsite we could find. Each of us set to work unloading the wet gear, setting up tents, and gathering wood for a fire.

Later that evening, we lay out all the food on a tarp and assessed the situation. It did not look good. Because we failed to pack all of the food in watertight containers, much of it was lost. We opened the soggy box of pancake mix. What was to serve as two of our breakfasts was now a pile of bread dough. The box of macaroni and cheese met much the same fate. The noodles were mushy and stuck together. The only items that were spared were the Pop-Tarts, a dozen hot dogs, some instant oatmeal, a few Snickers bars, and some bouillon cubes.

"Pretty slim pickings," Pat said with a laugh.

"Sure is. We're gonna be one hungry bunch before this trip is through," Pete added.

After a bit more discussion, we quickly surmised it was not nearly enough food to sustain all four of us for the remainder of the trip. Unless someone could demonstrate some sort of hidden animal-snaring skills, it was clear two of us would have to turn around and go back home. While we were only a one-day paddle in, we were still a solid three-day paddle away from our intended finish point. Add to that a day's travel back home and the writing was clearly on the wall. Doug wanted no part in turning back, so he and Pat offered to continue on. Pete and I, our dignity already in the tank, said we would turn back after a night's rest. Once the decision was made, we got a fire started and roasted hot dogs for dinner. Before we settled into our tents for the night, we hung up our wet clothes and equipment to dry on clotheslines.

That night we got a nice rain.

Parting Our Ways

The next morning, we woke to our sodden camp and all of the bleakness that comes with a wet forest and an undetermined breakfast menu. The overnight rain, added to equipment which was already soaked, was the final nail in the coffin for me. It was a toxic mix of bad planning, poor decisions, and adverse conditions, and it did me in. My spirit was broken. I was not prone to giving up, and when it came to outdoor activities, I liked to boast about my ability to deal with adversity. This trip was different. It had a humiliating edge to it, and it defeated me. I was done.

Pete and I awoke, got dressed in the driest clothes we had, and met Pat and Doug for a hearty breakfast of granola bars. We broke camp immediately after in order to get a jump on the day. Pete and I plotted our route back, while Doug and Pat set a goal for the day's travel in the opposite direction. We divided up the remaining food as appropriately as we could based on what lay ahead of each pair. Pete and I took a couple Pop-Tarts and a few Snicker bars, and Doug and Pat claimed the rest. They had a much longer itinerary than us but seemed confident they could finish the trip with the remaining food. The one intangible was the potential of a fish dinner, but given that neither of them was much of a fisherman, they knew that was a long shot. We said our goodbyes, wished each other good luck, and parted ways. There were no hard feelings, and, frankly, if our food had been spared, we would have made a go of it.

Pete and I paddled back upriver with vigor. When we reached the rapids that had done us in the day before, we pulled over and portaged. On the other side, we started paddling back using the same route we had come by. Paddling upstream is much harder than going with the current, but we knew we didn't have terribly far to go. We worked well together, determined to avoid making any mistakes like we made the day before. The locations of the portages were still fresh in our minds and that made it easy to keep on track.

After a few hours, we were back on Gunflint Lake. Although we were just there the day before, it really felt like a week. So much had transpired in a single day. Everything—the leaky canoe, Doug's illness, getting lost, and our eventual whitewater disaster—was just a lot to have been through in a single day. It was like a weeklong Outward Bound experience compressed into twenty-four hours. The whole debacle scared me straight in terms of respecting the forces of nature.

Because Gunflint Lake serves as an entry point into Boundary Waters, development is permitted and there is a well-known resort on the lake called Gunflint Lodge. We pointed the canoe in the direction of the lodge and paddled hard. We landed and went in to use the phone, trying not to look defeated in the process. The lobby was modern and comfortable, with knotty pine paneling, hardwood floors, and a few stuffed trophy fish on the walls. We got the number for Seagull Outfitters, called, and told them we needed to be picked up.

"You weren't supposed to be coming out until Friday," the owner said with surprise in his voice.

"Uh, yeah, we had a little mishap in the rapids and we were forced to split up," Pete explained.

"Okay. Someone will be there in half an hour."

When the driver arrived, we helped load the canoe and gear and climbed in the van. After describing our experience to the driver, no one said much on the ride back to the outfitter. When we arrived and ambled in, our clothes were finally dry from the morning's travel. "You guys had some trouble, I heard," the proprietor said.

"Yeah, first we got lost and then we capsized in the rapids by Pine Island," Pete said.

"What were you doing shooting *those* rapids? Those are pretty intense!"

"Well, we were lost and being lazy. The whole thing is a long story," I added.

"Where are the other guys?"

"They're finishing up and should be in by Friday,"

His eyes widened and his eyebrows rose. "You left them out there?"

"Uh, yeah, they wanted to finish the trip out," I said.

He didn't seem to share our nonchalance. It was as if he thought we left them for dead or something. We realized that, as an outfitter, it was part of this guy's job to see to it that his patrons returned, but we were also confident that if Pat and Doug were committed to something, they would complete it. They had the option to turn back and made the choice not to. We couldn't force them, no matter what we felt their chances were. He obviously questioned our judgment, but it really was out of our control at that point.

"The bad news is we did some damage to your canoe that we need to square up with you, too," I added.

"Let's go have a look at it," the owner said.

We filed outside and gathered around the wounded boat. The owner looked at the popped rivets and gave us an estimate of about fifty dollars to fix it. We thought that was fair, so we added an additional twenty-five dollars each to the total expenses for the trip. We paid him, apologized again, picked up our packs, and started walking down the Gunflint Trail.

As light as the traffic is on the highway coming into the Boundary Waters, it is even lighter when you're at the northernmost end of it heading back south. There we were, starting our way back in much the same way as we had come up—on foot and swatting bugs all the way.

One of the casualties of our tango with the rapids was the frame of my backpack. The upright six inches of metal frame had broken off. The piece served to hold the flap that pulled over the top of my sleeping bag and secured it on top of my clothes. Because it was broken, the sleeping bag worked itself loose and it hung out to one side and flopped like a backpack hernia. Every quarter mile or so, I had to ask Pete to push it back in so it wouldn't fall out entirely. After about four or five times doing this, Pete's patience began to wear thin. He was toting his own heavy Duluth pack and was tired of having to babysit mine.

"Dude, you have to do something about this bag thing. It's driving me nuts," Pete said.

"Sorry, man. This pack's going in the trash when I get home," I said with a laugh.

We walked for quite a while in long stretches of silence with nothing but the sounds of our boots crunching on the gravel shoulder. Parasitic gnats orbited our heads in dense flocks, occasionally landing and taking a chunk of us for their trip back home. The physical exertion combined with the heat and the lack of fresh water was causing both of us to become dehydrated. Back at the outfitter we bought a two-liter bottle of Sprite, but we gulped it down greedily early on our journey back down the trail. It was gone now, and there was no fresh water in sight, at least in the near future.

Occasionally a car droned by, its riders ignoring our pleading thumbs. It was glaringly clear now that the whole hitchhiking portion of the travel plan was one that had great allure and mystique on paper but was confoundingly frustrating in practice. It was difficult to plan anything very far ahead if you didn't know where you'd be at the end of every day.

It was early afternoon and my thirst began to dominate my thoughts. Part of the obsession came from not knowing how far it was to some source of fresh water, whether it was a lodge, a store, or even a stranger's cabin. The other part was fueled by not knowing when, or if, we would ever catch a ride. Combined, the thoughts rolled around my dry skull as I plodded forward one step at a time.

By a stroke of dumb luck, when our thirst was reaching its zenith, we approached a small creek that passed alongside the highway. Pete and I couldn't resist and stepped off the road to take a closer look. It wasn't much more than a large spring, really, maybe two feet across at its widest point. The stream's water was clear and the bottom sandy. I cupped a small handful of the cool water and brought it up to my mouth and slurped it in. It was divine. The hint of metallic taste was more than worth the satisfaction the water provided. The two of us gulped just enough to satisfy our immediate thirst and not much more. We saw the results of wild-water overindulgence firsthand with Doug the day before and wanted no part of it.

After our refreshing break at the creekside cantina, we resumed our hitchhiking and walking. About thirty minutes later, a car pulled over shortly after it passed us. We ran to the car and climbed into the back seat. As luck would have it, the campers who picked us up were going all the way to Grand Marais. Finally, a travel event that was in our favor! We sat back and enjoyed the hour-and-a-half ride to the bottom of the trail.

The car came to a stop at the junction of the trail and Highway 61, which was our route back to Duluth. We jumped out and thanked the driver for making our day. Relieved to be on a busier highway, we started walking down the shoulder, showing our thumbed salutes.

We were at it no more than ten minutes before a US Immigration patrol car pulled over in front of us. The brown-clad officer got out, slammed his door, and ambled up to us. "Good afternoon, gentlemen. Where you boys from?" he inquired.

"Uh, St. Paul, sir," Pete answered.

"That where you're headed?"

"Yep, sure is," Pete said.

He asked to see our IDs and we obligingly pulled out our driver's licenses and passed them to him. He took a quick look, verified we weren't border-jumping Canadians, and gave them back to us.

"Alright, you boys have a good day, and best of luck getting a ride," he said.

"Thanks, we'll need it," I joked.

The officer drove away, evidently unwilling to carry us farther away from the border. It wasn't more than twenty minutes later that a big roomy sedan pulled over and waved us up. We were somewhat surprised to find it was a woman who was probably in her sixties. Experience had shown us that people who picked us up usually tended to be males under fifty years old. Of course, we were harmless, but no one else knew that. This woman was either a good judge of character or just a kind soul.

"Hey, thanks for the lift," I said. I threw my pack in the back seat and climbed in up front. Pete took off his pack, set it next to mine, and jumped in back.

The woman had grey hair and thick, plastic-rimmed glasses. She was sweet and had a hardened, self-sufficient look about her face. This look and demeanor comes from living in the rugged Arrowhead region of Minnesota. Decades of living among blizzards, woods, and bugs tends to toughen the character of people up there. They are good people, and their independent spirit is worn with pride on their unassuming exteriors. If they should slide into a ditch in a snowstorm, they're more likely to die trying to push the car out themselves than to ask for help.

It turned out she was headed all the way to Duluth, so we lucked out again. We passed the time with small talk and recounting our adventure of the previous couple days. During our conversation, it struck me how similar people are when it comes right down to it. Here we were sharing our lives with a complete stranger, provoked by a totally random meetup, yet we were able to relate like we were her grandsons. Long stretches of road have a way of peeling people's lives open like Clementine oranges.

The drive to Duluth took about two and a half hours. Our driver was kind enough to go out of her way and drop us off at the Amtrak station. We thanked her, grabbed our packs, and went inside. Still dehydrated from the trip down the trail and the long car ride, the two of us made a beeline for the snack counter. I slurped down a Pepsi and then a second, thinking I would *never* again take the sweet goodness of a cold soda for granted. Furthermore, I vowed never to plan so poorly that I would reach that stage of dehydration again.

We were fortunate enough to get tickets for the next train to St. Paul with the little remaining money we had left. When the train arrived, we checked our backpacks, boarded, and headed back to the civilized world we knew as home.

Doug and Pat eventually made it home safely as well. They had some great stories. They told of living on bouillon soup on the last day. They laughed about encroaching on another canoe's fishing area in hopes that they would catch some of what they were missing out on. And they relayed how they spent a night on the cold, damp shores of Lake Superior when they couldn't manage a ride out of Grand Marais. Not to discount my own story, but theirs was the real adventure. We were survivors of the same voyage, just taken on different courses.

This trip was a mixed blessing. It served as a rite of passage for us as high school grads—a chance to flee the nest and stretch our wings a bit. We were out to assert our independence and prove ourselves. Our attempts went belly-up early and, as it turned out, we did everything wrong. We broke some cardinal rules, made poor on-the-fly decisions, and generally took a cocky, arrogant approach going in. What we got out of it was a good old-fashioned Mother Nature butt kick.

As disappointing as the trip was for me, it served to set the stage for how I would approach my future trips to the area. I learned much more from the failures and "snafus" encountered than I did in all the subsequent trips combined. I am convinced it turned out poorly for a reason. In my case, it did not squelch my love of the outdoors. It only made me determined to learn from my mistakes and try again. Despite the way the trip ended, Pat and I made a pact to redo the entire route the correct way. We had to prove it could be done right.

The Fix-It Trip

In the spring of 1980, Pat and I talked about making the trip up and retracing the route of the year before. Pete and Doug expressed no interest in reliving the ordeal, having had more than enough the year before. I personally felt embarrassed by the outcome and knew I was capable of better. Pat and I, from a friendship standpoint, were probably the closest of the four, so even though he had finished the trip, he agreed we should try it again. It seemed he had some deep-seated pride issues about it and wanted to correct the errors of our past. With better planning and many lessons learned, we were sure we could do it—and do it well.

I will admit that planning for a trip for two was considerably easier than one for four. A couple of rules we mutually agreed on were laid out right up front. The first was that if we came to any whitewater that posed even the slightest risk or danger, we would, at a minimum, portage our gear and take an empty canoe down. We were determined not to repeat the soggy food escapade of a year prior. Pat was intimately familiar with the diet of chicken-bouillon-cube soup and was determined not to relive it.

The second rule was that we would share the job of navigating. One of the mistakes we made on the prior trip was relying on Doug to do all the navigating. He had strong leadership tendencies, so we tended to take direction from him without question. I am not placing the blame on Doug for getting lost but rather on all of us for not working more by committee. A true democracy only works if you have a system of checks and balances.

Perhaps the most hugely significant difference between the trips was our mode of transportation. Pat said we should take his car rather than rely on a train, a bus, and our thumbs. He had acquired a 1955

Plymouth Belvedere from his aunt when she could no longer drive. We both realized having a car would take much of the guesswork and intangibles out of the trip and make it more affordable to boot.

The car was a classic beauty with only thirty-five thousand original miles on it. It was almost regal in its factory mint-green paint with a glossy white hardtop roof. The massive hood was crowned with a wingless silver jet-looking thing meant to imply a quickness the vehicle never had, even in its heyday. Its back seat could almost hold four adults, and Pat always joked that the trunk could sleep six. It wasn't far from the truth. The car was as big as a houseboat and, as I recall, handled every bit like one.

The chrome front grille and thick, heavy bumper were rounded and awkward looking, like misshapen automotive orthodontia. When paired with its chrome canopied headlights, the front end took on the endearing, innocent character of a robot face. The interior sported fabric- and vinyl-upholstered bench seats, a simple dash with AM radio, and small triangular "fly" windows commonly used to vent cigarette smoke. The steering wheel was enormous, with finger grips rippling on the underside and a chrome horn arcing in a band across the bottom third of the wheel. Oddly enough, the glove box was in the middle of the dash, necessitating that a couple of the indicator dials had to be placed on the passenger's side. It was a peculiar design, but as long as you had a passenger to tell you what your temp and volt gauges read, you were good to go.

Despite the car's generally good condition, it was not without quirks. The most notable was that the front passenger door handle didn't work. The push-button latch mechanism was broken to the point that the door simply would not open. Wherever we went, Pat would have to open the driver-side door and let me slide across the bench seat to the passenger side. He would then follow me into his spot in the driver's seat. Getting out would reverse the scenario, with him getting out his door and me following.

While this practice might seem acceptable, one might even say romantic, for a man and woman, for two guys it looked a little odd. People likely drew some pretty predictable conclusions about our sexual orientation based on our door ritual. Instead of worrying about it, we shelved our pride and even had a few laughs about the whole process at some of the stops along the way. It seemed like a small price to pay for good transportation.

When Pat acquired the car, it came complete with an ivory-colored plastic statue of St. Christopher, the Catholic patron saint of travelers. The statue had a magnetized base that held it to the metal dash. Pat kept it there out of respect for his aunt. At times, when we had close calls with an inattentive driver or a nearly empty gas tank, Pat would tap the statue on the head as an act of gratitude to St. Chris in case he was watching. Having it roost there on the dash gave the car an even more unique feel.

One of the problems of owning a vintage cruiser at the age of nineteen is that you quickly discover the expense of maintaining a classic. Old car parts were hard to find and expensive. Finding a mechanic willing to work on a twenty-five-year-old car was not easy, either. With expensive upkeep and the car's propensity for hogging gas, it quickly became a money pit for Pat.

Shortly after he got the car, a hole developed in the exhaust pipe that led into the muffler. As the hole grew larger over time, the noise increased. Eventually, the car roared like an F-14 fighter jet. It was positively earsplitting from the street and only mildly better inside the cab. When Pat looked into having it repaired before the trip, he found it would cost hundreds of dollars to replace the exhaust system. This was a problem, considering we were leaving on a long trip in a week. The thought of driving with the screaming muffler for five hours was not appealing to either of us.

His solution to the problem was to buy a "muffler bandage" kit for about ten dollars from the local 10,000 Auto Parts store. The kit included a tube of epoxy and a two-inch-wide roll of some sort of fiberglass-and-plastic composite material. Knowing his financial constraints, I embraced the solution as a decent plan B.

The day before we left, we applied the quick fix to the muffler. Outside Pat's garage, I guided as he drove the rumbling Plymouth onto the auto ramps he had for just this sort of situation. Pat crawled under the car and applied a liberal amount of epoxy and then wound the bandage in a cast-like manner around the offending rusted pipe. After letting it dry and adhere for twenty minutes, the only thing left to do was to see if it worked as well as it does "as seen on TV."

Pat climbed behind the steering wheel, put the key in in the ignition, and said, "Now, for the moment of truth." When he turned the key, the car cranked slowly to life and hummed with showroom quietness.

We did it! We smiled guilty grins at each other as if we had gotten away with something. I wondered why everyone didn't use these bandages. They seemed like a miracle cure that was too good to be true. We both knew it was the equivalent of a Band-Aid on an artery, but we were astounded at how simple and easy it was to quiet the beast. Happy with our fix, we agreed on a time to meet the next day and parted ways. It felt good to be starting our redemptive trip with a victory.

Plymouth Rock

Early the next afternoon, Pat arrived at my house in the Plymouth, which was all fueled and ready to go. I packed my gear into the trunk and, after taking a few steps toward my door, realized I had to enter through his side. I wheeled on my heel and walked around to the driver's side. With a laugh, Pat opened the door and said, "After you." He never missed a chance to crack me up when he saw one.

We found our way to the interstate and started toward the great northern wilderness. The sheer mass of the Plymouth and its strong, capable V-8 engine made freeway riding a pleasure. The ride was strangely quiet. We were used to the deafening roar of the bad pipe, so it was a nice change. I gazed out the window, excited for our coming adventure and content in knowing we only had a five-hour drive and not a full day of trains, buses, and hitchhiking like last year.

The car was equipped with only the standard tinny-sounding AM radio. Because all the good rock stations of the day were on the FM band, Pat packed a portable cassette player and radio to give us more control over what we listened to and to help pass the time. We were close friends and shared similar musical tastes: Springsteen, Jackson Browne, ZZ Top, and our favorite, George Thorogood. I popped a George cassette into the deck and we were off and rocking.

"*Ride on, Josephine, girl, you got a runnin' machine,*" George sang in his gravelly voice. We had our own runnin' machine and were happy to be on the road at last.

About twenty miles into the trip, the noise level in the car increased. It started as a quiet yet unmistakable hum. Pat and I exchanged a concerned glance. Within a few miles, the noise grew louder as the patch began to give way. The patch surrendered to the heat of the offending pipe, and before long we were right back to our pre-patch decibel level.

"Well, so much for that great idea, I guess," Pat said.

"Yeah, well, it was worth a shot, anyway."

As we continued on, we detected a faint smell of exhaust in the car. It was not overpowering but was noticeably present. We both cracked our windows a bit to keep the fresh air flowing. We knew the dangers of carbon-monoxide poisoning and took measures to avert a catastrophe.

The miles rolled away as we headed north in our mint-colored time machine. Somewhere near Two Harbors, Minnesota, we switched drivers. Pat had developed a headache and was looking to get a break from driving. I slid behind the enormous steering wheel and took my shift. As I cruised along, I began to obsess about the exhaust smell and its possible effects on us. My mind began its own little monologue.

Is that a headache I feel coming on?

Is the smell getting worse?

Pat's been asleep a long time. Is he breathing? I hope he's okay.

About a half hour later, Pat began to stir. *Good*, I thought, *he's not dead!* When he sat up and rubbed his eyes after his nap, I told him how I'd been worried that I'd killed him in a carbon-monoxide manslaughter. We both laughed at my admission. Sometimes on vacations, getting there is half the fun.

Lost with the Boss

When Pat and I arrived at the outfitters, we rented a canoe and told the clerk we needed transportation to our starting point. We planned on starting out on Gunflint Lake and canoeing a looping route, ending up at Seagull Outfitters as we did last year. The outfitter went over our route so he and the Forest Service knew roughly where we'd be on each day as we traveled. We strapped the rented aluminum Grumman canoe on the transport van and the driver delivered us to our starting launch pont at around seven o'clock in the evening.

The outfitter helped us set the canoe in the water. Pat and I loaded it up and were on our way. It felt good to be in the fresh air outside of a moving car and to be starting on our journey. We searched for a small inlet that led to Magnetic Lake. As we paddled, we didn't see any visible openings in the area where we thought the river should have been. We pushed on, thinking it must have been further ahead than we remembered. Soon dusk crept in and we started to think we wouldn't have a place to camp by nightfall.

Pat tried to lighten the mood by putting a tape in the player. He picked Bruce Springsteen's *Darkness on the Edge of Town* and pushed the play button. The song played at three-quarter speed. It seemed the batteries were nearly sapped of their charge, which left Bruce singing like he had a mouthful of molasses. Now, it's important to understand that the song "Darkness on the Edge of Town" played at *full* speed is somber enough to put a person to sleep. When you slow it down to the speed we were hearing it, it was a painful, haunting ballad that did nothing to lighten the mood. In fact, it did quite the opposite. Pat laughed as he switched off the Boss and said, "That's enough of that, then."

Dusk turned to darkness. Because we were on the fringe of the BWCA, not only were small motors allowed, but there were a few private cabins on the lake as well. As our situation grew increasingly dire, we spotted a light in the distance. Not having a better plan, we worked our way toward it. We thought we would see if it led us to someone who could get us reoriented on the lake.

Suddenly we heard the rumble of a two-stroke boat engine starting in the distance behind us. Its whine offended the quietness of night and slowly grew louder as it approached in the gloom. The green, red, and white running lights crept toward our canoe and I wondered if they realized they were not on the lake alone. We didn't have the required running lights and were traveling in a very dangerous stealth mode. As they passed us in a full-throttle wail about fifty yards away, Pat heard one of them say, "It's some stupid canoeists!"

Hey, I'd been called worse. Never in a canoe, of course, but worse.

We pried our way through the darkness and it wasn't long before we pulled our canoe up to the shore near the lighted cabin. The two of us walked around the place, looking for the door and hoping the owner didn't have a hunting rifle and an attitude. Back home, a person is used to people and solicitors visiting their residence. Up here, it was likely a rarity to get unexpected visitors after dark. We knocked on the door and, after a moment, a middle-aged man in jeans and a flannel shirt cautiously opened it.

"Can I help you?"

"Uh, yeah, actually. Could you tell us where we are on this map?" Pat asked as he opened the map.

"Hmm, let me see. Well, this is where I'm at." He pointed to a small rectangle and a dashed line on the map. "That's my driveway right there. Where are you guys headed?"

"We're trying to get to Magnetic Lake," I said.

He pointed to the inlet that was just a short paddle northwest of where we were.

"Yeah, looks like we went right past it and just kept going," I said.

"We really hate to bother you, but would it be okay with you if we set up our tent in your yard here?" Pat asked. We were both tired and hoped he would not make us return to our canoe and keep paddling in the dark.

"Sure, no problem. Anywhere out there is fine," he replied.

We lucked out by stumbling upon someone afflicted with "Minnesota Nice." People like him and the older woman who gave us a ride from Grand Marais to Duluth last year were testament to the condition. Pat and I thanked him and started putting up the tent in the back yard of the cabin. It was beginning to seem like the black cloud of mistakes that blanketed us the year before continued to follow us on this trip, too.

Making Up Time

We awoke the next morning to clear skies and a fresh outlook. Pat was especially optimistic and upbeat. He always had a positive attitude when it came to life's trials, and it was infectious. He was determined not to let last night's setback cast a pall over the rest of the trip. We had set out to prove we could do this trip, and the setback was not going to deter us. It did mean we would really have to hammer on the paddles to make up for lost time.

After a quick, simple breakfast, we loaded the canoe and started in the direction of Magnetic Lake. In the bright sunlight, the narrow opening leading to the lake was much more obvious. We laughed at how easy it was to spot and how our narrow miss cost us some time. We dipped our paddles deep and hard into Gunflint Lake, as we knew we had to make at least four portages to catch up to where we should be by the end of the day.

We passed through the channel leading to Magnetic Lake, which was much smaller than Gunflint. It felt good to be on a smaller body of water, and we were confident that we were finally headed in the right direction. Before long, we were across the lake and into the Pine River system. We had seen this stretch of the Pine before—in my case, going both directions—so we took it on with a bit of attitude.

When we came upon our first set of rapids, we approached them with caution and respect. We landed the canoe and surveyed what we were up against. The water rippled over a few large rocks but was flowing pretty well, so we decided to give it a shot. We climbed in, pushed off, and jockeyed the canoe deftly through the ripples, carefully avoiding all the big submerged boulders along the way.

"Woohoo!" Pat shouted after we passed through the small rapids. We high-fived each other using our paddles when the water smoothed out and slowed down. Whitewater always has a way of getting my adrenaline flowing, no matter how small the challenge.

The Pine and Granite Rivers that made up much of our route actually form the boundary between the United States and Canada. Scattered along the way were brass markers sitting in the middle of the river with "U.S." stamped on one side and "Canada" on the other. It was the closest thing to a Great Wall that our two countries ever needed. City slickers that we were, we occasionally paddled on the Canadian side just to be able to say we had been in Canada. In the middle of nowhere, we took those moments of entertainment when we could get them.

After a short lunch on shore, we pressed on into the afternoon's work. We looked at each set of rapids and made the choice as we went, erring on the side of caution if there was any doubt. The challenge of paddling whitewater has a dangerous attraction to it. We learned the hard way last year that this allure can have serious consequences if it isn't kept in check. So when we came to the fateful Pine Island Portage, it was never a question; we unpacked the gear and made the trek up the trail. It was a long, difficult hike since we were laden down with gear and boat, but it was time well spent given the events of the previous year. Since there were only two of us, making decisions proved much easier. Where two is company, three or four is either gridlock or anarchy.

We paddled on, taking shortcuts by shooting the simple rapids where we could. These shortcuts and some serious paddling enabled us to continually make up time from the day before. Pat and I loved being in God's country. The crystalline water allowed us to see right to the bottom along much of the Pine and Granite Rivers. Boulders rounded by hundreds of years of hard-flowing water decorated the river bottom. Their colors of iron red, slate grey, and spotted ivory made each one unique, and together they formed a dazzling geological jumble. Fallen trees, stripped of all but the nubs where branches once were, appeared to be thrust into the water by storms and winds of the past. Occasionally we passed a freshly fallen pine or birch, its leaves and branches bending obediently to the water's current. It felt good to be going with the current as well.

By dusk, we made our way out of the Granite River system and found a decent campsite on Devil's Elbow Lake, so named for the wicked hairpin turn that shaped it. We were both exhausted from the hard day. In all, we covered five portages and more than eight miles on the water.

After gathering firewood and setting up our tent, we started a fire and set about making dinner—Hamburger Helper alfresco. This time, we packed the beef in a block of ice and carried it in a cooler. It was still rock solid when we started dinner. We learned our lesson from the blonde-hamburger episode of the year before and were careful not to make the same mistake twice. Once the hamburger browned, we mixed in the noodles, water, and seasoning packet. To a couple of tired canoeists, it looked like a poor man's version of Mom's Hot Dish goodness. Within minutes, we finished the whole pan as well as a piece of bread with butter.

Shortly after dinner, I felt a roiling in my gut. It was one of those episodes you just know will not end well. I started down the toilet trail as my mouth began to water in that familiar way. After a few yards, I wretched and spilled my still-warm dinner and what felt like a couple of nonvital organs into the woods. In computer talk, it was what is known as a warm boot. After a couple small dry-heave "aftershocks," I tottered back to camp.

"I just puked my dinner," I confessed.

Pat chuckled. "Really? Feeling better?"

"A little bit, now," I replied.

"What happened, man?"

"I think I'm just so exhausted my stomach wasn't ready for what I threw at it," I answered. I sat on a nearby log, poured a cup of water from the canteen and took a sip. One of the few benefits that come from losing your lunch is that you always feel better afterwards. We went to bed shortly after dark and made it an early night. In the morning, I was back to normal and more than ready to tackle day three.

Getting in a Rhythm

Because we made up so much lost time the day before, we decided we could relax a bit on day three. We did a little fishing and explored the area. In doing so, we found a much more desirable campsite and decided to move there and spend the night. It was a spectacular site on the lower part of Maraboef Lake. It had a level site for the tent with a soft bed of pine needles as well. The canoe landing was gently sloped and had a nice vista of the lake, which afforded a gentle breeze off the water to keep the bugs at bay. It turned out our hardworking effort of the day before paid off after all, allowing us to take advantage of one of the prettiest sites I've ever camped at.

The next morning, day four, we woke up and made a breakfast of bacon and pancakes. This meal finished off our bacon, and with the rest of our meat also consumed, we were able to discard the remnants of the block of ice we still had left in the cooler. We both marveled at the difference between this trip, in which we had ice until the last day, and last year's, in which it was completely melted by the end of day one. We were beginning to recognize how far we had come, from a planning standpoint, based on our disastrous experience the year before.

After breakfast, we resumed our hard paddling. At this point, we were still on schedule but needed to cover some decent distance to stay on it. We set off and worked northward on Maraboef Lake. When we got to Horsetail Rapids, we got out and assessed them. They appeared to both of us to be harmless, so we climbed in and shot them without incident. It was a nice adrenaline rush, and we high-fived with our paddles again to celebrate. A short distance later we came upon Saganaga Falls. Again we pulled over to take a look.

The falls were not terribly steep, but the water was high and they churned with tenacity. We took a few minutes to admire them and watch the water take its course. Whitewater mesmerizes and fascinates with its power. It billows and rages, morphs and evolves. It lives. It is both soothingly hypnotic and unnervingly terrifying at the same time. You look deep into it, hoping to find its nucleus and heart but only discovering it is a beast with many heads — a Hydra. It is not to be understood but to be feared, respected, and revered.

After our ten-minute scenic break, we portaged around the falls and got back on the water. We continued north, and at Conner's Island we began to work our way westward. Suddenly, things became confusing on the map. A multitude of closely spaced small islands resided in the area, and trying to determine which was which often involved a bit of guesswork. After a little discussion, it became apparent that by hugging tight to the southern shoreline on the left side of the canoe, we couldn't go too far astray. We knew it might add some time to the trip, but we wouldn't get lost. We had our one setback and were determined not to repeat it.

The area was gorgeous country with numerous available camping spots on many of the islands. We worked hard, and toward late afternoon we thought it was prudent to get settled for the night. We headed for a site on Schlei Island. When we landed, I told Pat that as long as we were there, I had to go find the toilet. He said he had to take a leak and wandered off toward the trees, while I grabbed the toilet paper and headed toward the commode.

When we returned, we were talking about how much we didn't like this island at all. I spat to one side. Just as I did, Pat let out an echoing fart that cracked both of us up. I pointed out that since we'd done almost everything excretory we were capable of, it was probably a sign we should leave the island.

"Schnay on Schlei," I said.

"Yep, schnay on Schlei," Pat agreed.

We both started laughing uncontrollably. It was one of the things I loved the most about Pat. The two of us had very similar senses of humor, and when we jelled, unbridled insanity ensued.

Schnay was a word we and a couple other high school friends made up as seniors, and it carried on into our college years. Simply put, it meant an emphatic *no*. Teens do strange things like making up their own dialects sometimes, and this was part of ours. In school we often strung the word out and made it come across almost as multiple syllables. "Ssssscccchhhhnnnnaaaayyyyy!" The additional emphasis relayed the message quite clearly to the listener that the speaker was serious about his objections.

Having defiled Schlei Island and agreeing that it was not worthy of a night's stay, we ambled back to the canoe and paddled on. We weaved our way between clusters of small islands and eventually settled for a much nicer site on Horseshoe Island.

Since the island had a U shape, its naming actually made sense. But it caused me to wonder how the thousands of lakes, rivers, and islands in the area got their names. Many, I'm sure, were named for their geographic makeup. Devil's Elbow Lake, for example, made sense because it made an almost hairpin turn back on itself and actually looked a bit like an elbow. Cross Bay looked like a cross. Rocky Point spoke for itself.

It was the nondescript lake names that made me wonder how they got their titles. For example, what was the significance behind the names Gunflint Lake or Magnetic Lake? How about Ernest Lake, a small creek-fed lake off the beaten path? Did Ernest the voyageur happen upon it and claim it for himself? Or maybe it was just randomly assigned by the US Forest Service because they were in the "E" names on that particular day.

The list of odd names goes on and on. Burntside, Reward, Shadow, Prayer, Pogo, Squat, Pellet, Ambush, and Rally all beg the question, how did they earn their names? And just what is the history behind Romance Lake anyway? How about Skin Dance Lake? Or, better yet, Ashdick Lake? Cherry Lake looks nothing like a cherry, and Toe Lake looks more like a hammer toe than anything else. In the neighboring Canadian Quetico region, This Man Lake is not to be outdone by Other Man Lake to its north, and both are bigger than No Man's Lake to their south. Evidently Canadian cartographers had a sense of humor as well.

Finishing What We Started

After our one-night stay on Horseshoe Island, we broke camp and started out on the last major leg of our journey. We turned south on Saganaga Lake, a huge body of water along the Canadian border, and headed toward Open Channel, which led to Gull Lake. Our excitement rose as we began to see other canoeists and the first signs of civilization in five days.

Coming across other canoeists in the BW felt bittersweet. On the one hand, the social side of me welcomed the sight of new faces and I responded with requisite waves and hellos. On the other hand, the selfish part of me was resentful that they thrust themselves into my personal outdoor space. I always heard stories of people who went for days without seeing anyone. It was my feeling that if I saw others, no matter where, it took away from the trip and made it seem less isolated or exclusionary. After all, I didn't come to this area to be around people. If I wanted people, I'd go to the mall. I was a BWCA purist, and that meant one thing: minimal contact.

We paddled across Gull Lake to what would be our last portage. It was also the strangest portage on our journey since it traversed a road and a parking lot that served as the terminus of the Gunflint Trail. Lifting the canoe and trekking over a fully paved road felt a bit dissatisfying after having successfully navigated so many portages where the trail was uneven and difficult to cross. The sight of a few parked cars in the lot made it painfully obvious our trip was nearly complete.

We set the canoe into Seagull Lake and carefully packed the equipment into it. We climbed in and paddled to the nearest campsite on Fishhook Island, a J-shaped island that fit its name perfectly. We feasted on our remaining food. One of the pleasures of the last night of any camping trip was the buffet that took place in order to minimize the food you had to take home. Strange combinations and weird multicourse meals ruled the day. Dinner might have consisted of macaroni and cheese served in pita bread with a cup of oatmeal and a broken Pop-Tart. Meals were designed around whatever most significantly lightened the load. What Pat and I shared that night is long forgotten, but I do know we ate, and we ate heartily.

"This beats the bouillon soup Doug and I had for dinner about this time last year," Pat said.

"That's a fact. We've come a long way since then, eh?" I replied.

"Yep, sure have. Cheers," he said, nodding. We both took a swig of hot chocolate from our cups in a toast to our success.

The next morning, we headed for Seagull Outfitters, a short paddle from where we camped the night before. We pulled into the landing, got out, and high-fived each other. We did it! The disastrous trip from a year earlier could finally be put to rest. In some ways it was more meaningful to me, because Pat finished the trip with Doug the year before, whereas I had not. I needed to prove to myself I could do a trip and do it right.

No doubt, mistakes were made, but I think mistakes happen on *any* trip. The key is to minimize them. Big mistakes can be trip killers. Our efforts on this trip were focused on keeping the canoe upright, keeping our clothes and equipment dry, and packing the right food the right way. The fact that we arrived well rested, on schedule, and with food left over was proof our efforts paid dividends.

I think the success of this trip was due in large part to the fact that I took it with Pat, someone I considered my best friend. With just two of us, decisions were much simpler. A competitive mentality of "us versus them" did not exist as it sometimes did on the trip before. Our adventure together further solidified the friendship Pat and I share today, and I am grateful for having gone through it with him. Together we had paddled through the "Darkness on the Edge of Town" and had come back into the light.

Hitchin' a Ride

On our way back to St. Paul, Pat and I happened upon a hitchhiker near Sandstone, Minnesota. Having been on the begging end of enough hitchhiking, Pat stopped the rumbling Plymouth and waved the guy up. He ran up to the car and jumped in the back seat.

"Hey, thanks for the ride, guys," he said. He was an older man, probably in his forties.

"Sure, no problem," Pat replied.

As with most hitchhiking conversations, we proceeded to make small talk as a group for about twenty miles or so. When we finished with the pleasantries and talk of the weather, everyone quieted down for lack of anything better to talk about. Just about that time, the guy asked a question Pat and I still laugh about today.

"Hey, this is a great car, but do you guys ever get headaches driving in this thing?"

All the time, man. All the time.

Part II: Brothers

The Planning

I don't know for certain, but it's a fair guess the decision my brothers and I made to take a trip to the Boundary Waters Canoe Area happened over a beer. Though I moved to the Milwaukee metro area later, I was born and raised in Minnesota, and the trips I made back home usually entailed hanging out with my brothers, having a few beers, and talking smart. During our college years we became closer as siblings and as friends. Tom, my elder by six years, helped mentor me through my early college days, when my grades suffered because I couldn't seem to apply myself. He urged me to stick around after my morning classes to study before I went to work at four o'clock rather than go home by noon and fall victim to the many distractions there. I took his advice and, eventually, my grades climbed back up. While we didn't hang out much during our college years, he was always there, setting the example for me.

Paul, Rob, and I were closer in age and single, unlike Tom, so we socialized together a fair amount. This was not a slight against Tom in any way, just a difference in focuses during the years before the three of us ended up marrying, too. I won't deny, however, that the first few trips to the BWCA with Rob and Paul were an effort by us as younger brothers to forge our own way without Tom's tutelage. When we were younger, he taught us much of what we needed to know about camping and fishing and, in some senses, we were out to prove we could do it on our own. I'm fairly certain Tom understands this now, but it probably stung a bit at the time. While the three of us got along very well on the trips we took in the late '80s, in 1990, when Tom came with us, it proved that the *four* of us could get along just as well.

Tom was the oldest sibling; next in line came my three sisters: Pat, Linda, who died at age five of cancer, and Jane, who was just a year older than me. I was next, breaking the streak of girls, much to my father's satisfaction. Rob and Paul came shortly after and rounded out the mob. With seven kids born inside of ten years, it was a nice big Catholic family, raised by our mother, Mary, after my father's death in 1967. Our family was always extremely close. We saw each other through good times and bad, thick and thin. In fact, the entire family still keeps in touch despite being spread over three states. There are no outcasts or black sheep.

Shortly after graduating from the University of Minnesota, I took a job at a mapping firm in Minneapolis. I was laid off ten months later and moved back home with my mother while living on unemployment and looking for a job. That fall, a job opportunity came up in Waukesha, Wisconsin, near Milwaukee. Being close to my family, this was a tough move for me, but desperate times called for desperate measures, and I made the move to Waukesha in the fall of 1986.

While living in Wisconsin, I still managed to make regular trips back to Minnesota for holidays and special occasions. It was during one of these homecoming gatherings in 1987 that the subject of vacation came up. I do not recall where, but one of the local taverns on Grand Avenue in St. Paul is a good guess. Although most of the family lived out in the suburbs now, there was still the pull of the old neighborhood that kept us coming back. Grand Avenue was made up of an eclectic mix of retail and residential and, at the time, was a very popular nightspot area for people of our age group.

In talking the vacation idea through, the BWCA became the obvious destination. We all shared an appreciation for the outdoors and knew the potential for adventure the area held. Also at play, perhaps, was the undercurrent of nostalgia, knowing our father took trips like it on a few occasions with one or more of his brothers. None of us three younger boys ever really knew our dad—I was only five years old when he died—but we all heard stories and saw pictures of him, usually with a paddle, fishing rod, or hunting rifle in his hand. My sisters were older and knew him better, but they were not big campers or canoeists, so their attendance never came into the equation. These trips with my brothers were male-only affairs and may have been a subconscious effort in some way to rekindle our dad's spirit by retracing his footsteps.

Ultimately, it doesn't matter *where* the idea originated. The important thing is that it *did* and it continued long enough to create some magnificent memories. In '91, for no singular reason, the tradition sputtered and died. It may have been the onset of our marriages, the increasing demands of our careers, or just our choice to use vacation time in other ways. It's my feeling that part of the breakdown may have stemmed from too much togetherness. We got along pretty well most years, but after doing it five in a row, maybe the familiarity just bred contempt.

The first three years, the outings were comprised of Rob, Paul, our friend Keith, and me. Keith is an African-American friend Rob met in college when they were both attending the National Technical Institute for the Deaf in Rochester, New York. He and Rob are both hard of hearing and built up a tremendous friendship during those college years in the mid-80s. Keith relocated to the Twin Cities after college, in large part because of his friendship with Rob. Being so far from his family back home in Washington, D.C., we took him under our wing and he became like a brother to all of us.

The last couple trips of 1990 and 1991 were larger affairs in which the group grew to fill a third canoe. Combinations of our brother Tom and a couple of Paul's friends, Brad and John, were used in an effort to breathe some new life into the group. Brad was an even-keeled, industrious engineering graduate and John was a wily, boisterous college "tweener" —namely, between college and not-college.

It was the first few trips, however, that were the raw ones. We were learning the ropes, improvising, and perfecting our methods. In the process, we waded through our personality differences and idiosyncrasies and began establishing our roles. For example, early on it was determined that everyone would take part in the navigation. Each of us knew the difficulty in reading and following the maps as well as the danger of pinning the task on a single person. By spreading out the duty, it prevented any one person taking the blame in the event we got lost. If we got lost, it was *everyone's* fault.

Another upfront role-defining decision was that we agreed we would share the task of meal preparation. Just because Paul was the best cook of the four of us and seemed to enjoy the job didn't mean he should have to prepare dinner every night. We were all single males, so cooking was often kept fast and simple. In this respect, the camping menu fit quite well with what we were used to; if it couldn't be made in a stew pot or a skillet, it couldn't be made.

We had no set plan for the route we would take on our first trip. Each of us had been to the area before. Paul and I had gone on independent trips with our high school buddies, while Rob and Keith had gone as counselors for Courage North, a camp for kids with disabilities. Frankly, Rob and I were fairly indifferent to where we went, as long as it was somewhere remote and away from the big city. My only request, based on my previous history, was that we focus on lakes rather than whitewater. I had developed a thing for calm and serene water.

Without too much argument, we eventually agreed on a route Paul took a couple years earlier. We would start at the Mudro Lake entry point. He assured us it was safe and we could push as hard as we wanted and still have plenty of chances to fish and relax. It served as our starting point for a couple of years before we decided to change things up. The last few years we took a different route that started us on Snowbank Lake, about twenty miles outside of Ely.

As was our usual practice after choosing a route, very little happened in the way of planning until virtually the night before we left. Despite the fact that everyone except me lived within ten miles of each other, trip details managed to surface only via rumor or hearsay. Being the "out-of-towner," I typically drove up to St. Paul from Milwaukee the night before we were to leave. Then the serious planning would commence at "ground zero" in the family room of Mom's house. She was always very supportive of us taking the trip and was happy to oblige our planning and subsequent packing frenzies.

These ad-hoc planning gatherings would drive organized personalities to the brink of insanity. Significant details, like who was driving or how many days we were staying, were never decidedly concrete in advance. Those decisions were kicked around, hashed out, and finalized during the sessions in the family room. What we lacked in preparatory urgency we made up for in "cool." There wasn't much tolerance for uptightness anywhere along the trip, including the organizational process. As my wife will attest, my side of the family is known for being laid back, and these trips were no exception.

Also of note is that these trips all took place before the advent of cell phones, e-mail, or the internet. Any kind of collaboration was done using traditional phones. Because Rob and Keith had difficulty on the phone, and I was up against long-distance charges, things were best communicated face-to-face. With all of these variables at play, we chose to use the manic family-room planning sessions as a chance to build excitement for the adventure before us. To us, a good plan was a fresh plan.

The Packing

Once we had a plan and everyone was together, we hashed out the equipment and packing details. We discussed everything we were bringing, from clothes to fishing tackle to the latest camping gadget one of us acquired. Particulars, from obscurities—how many rolls of toilet paper were needed—to specifics—where the maps and compass would be stored—were worked out over a couple of beers in a Martha Stewart meets Keith Richards sort of way.

With the equipment technicalities addressed, our thoughts turned to menu planning and purchasing of food for the week. Anyone who has camped knows that much of it is centered on what the next meal is going to be. Being outdoors, your body kicks your metabolism up a notch and you start burning calories furiously. As food planner by default, Paul always made sure we ate heartily all week. During our first shopping trip, he took charge and loaded up the grocery cart with what appeared to be twice as much as we needed. Aisle by aisle, the cart slowly filled to bursting point. Rob and I frequently glanced at each other with raised eyebrows and shook our heads. We were ever conscious about our budgets and were thinking there was no way humanly possible we could eat that much food. Late in the week, as we pawed our way through the food pack, eating the second half of those same items, Rob and I were quick to compliment "our" shopping foresight.

Grocery-shopping ventures were usually conducted in the wee hours of the night before the trip. Since we all wanted input into what we were going to eat, we piled into Rob's car and drove over to Rainbow Foods, a twenty-four-hour grocery store. In the presence of glowing fluorescent lights, shiny waxed floors, and the wretched Muzak of bygone Barry Manilow and Rod Stewart songs, we joined the after-ten crowd in the supermarket. We blended in well with the underdressed, the insomniacs, and the nonconformists who chose to shop after the late news. To be fair, it was not a pretty sight—four twenty-something-year-old men prowling the aisles, quibbling about buying name-brand or generic, Skippy or Peter Pan. Suffice it to say, given our poor propensity for planning, coupons were not used.

On our maiden shopping trip, Paul dropped a king-sized can of Surfin' Berry Kool-Aid into the cart.

"Surfin' Berry?" Rob asked.

Paul stuck his hands out and struck his best surfer pose and said, "It goes with the water theme. You have to stay hydrated and ready to surf!"

We all laughed, amused by the entertaining drink choice he had made. I suddenly conjured up visions in my head of the Kool-Aid man crashing through the forest trees, saying, "Oh yeah!!!"

Our next stop was the bulk dry-goods aisle, where we surveyed the ingredients for trail mix. When you are on the move in a canoe, hunger sneaks up on you and you reach for something quick, easy, and filling. Trail mix, comprised of M&M's, raisins, peanuts, pretzels, and freeze-dried fruit, made for the perfect solution to these hunger spells. It's high in carbohydrates and provides a nice sugar boost as well. We packed a few pounds of it every year and it never went to waste. It was a camp favorite.

We grabbed a plastic bag and then doubled it up so it wouldn't spill if it was torn. A healthy ratio of chocolate, protein, carbohydrates, and salty ingredients was thrown in. When Paul dumped in a scoop of dried bananas, Rob and I passed a glance between us and raised our eyebrows. Next, he grabbed a small prepackaged bag of dried apricots. Rob, being more vocal than me and being concerned that a good trail mix was being fruited up, questioned Paul's choice.

"Apricots?"

"Yeah, apricots," Paul answered. "They keep you regular, if you know what I mean."

Rob shook his head, grinned, and pushed the cart onward. I had to give Paul credit. While they may not have been our group's ingredient of choice, I think he put forth a convincing argument in the idea of regularity. Despite being the youngest, Paul sometimes had a persuasive sensibility that was hard to argue with.

As we cruised the aisles, our cart slowly filled with pasta, ramen noodles, potatoes, granola bars, Rice-A-Roni, and instant oatmeal. This was followed by pancake mix, pita bread, squirt-top butter, fish breading, and of course, Pop-Tarts. At the time it seemed excessive, but it always worked out just about right. I cannot recall a trip with the brothers in which the food pack was missing something or any of us went to bed hungry. This was a pleasant change from the high school trip years before, during which we were a day short of resorting to making stone tools for hunting and gathering.

After about an hour and a half of shopping, we'd begin to lose interest and steer the heavy-laden cart for the checkout counter. A couple of us unloaded while the other two bagged the goods. As the register tape got longer, we passed nervous glances back and forth. It became obvious we might have made the mistake of shopping when we were hungry. When the total rang up, we dropped our jaws and reached for our wallets. Because it was early enough in the trip, most of us had the money. On occasion, someone came up short or concocted some lame excuse for not having his share and was usually granted a short-term loan until the next day.

At this stage of the trip, we were a peaceable group. On-the-spot loans and financial amnesty were doled out freely. The end of the week was a different story. Fiscal accusations, alibis, and outright falsehoods flew around the group with increasing frequency. Verbal promissory notes agreed upon earlier in the week were suddenly forgotten by their debtors as though the fresh air and lake water caused short-term memory loss. Much of the settling up was done with tit-for-tat financing deals, often rounded to the nearest five dollars. "I'll cover you when we get to a cash machine in town" became the plea bargain of the week. The debtor would then receive a daily gentle reminder from the lending party to keep them honest. To this day, I think there are a few unsettled debts between us.

Every year, when the shopping was done, we loaded the groceries into the trunk of Rob's car and returned to Mom's house to pack them and the rest of our gear. These sessions involved short bursts of packing, lots of oversight, and a decent amount of standing around and drinking beer. The beer drinking often fostered the excessive oversight, which then served to hinder the packing process. It was a highly dysfunctional workflow, but it set the tone for the rest of the week. I believe that is why there is no beer drinking during business hours in the working world. Everyone becomes an expert with a beer in their hand.

One thing that did get carried out with religious fervor was waterproofing the food. The dry goods, regardless of what they were packaged in, were put into Ziploc bags. To save space, boxed meals were put into Ziplocs, and their cooking instructions were ripped off and included so we weren't left guessing how to prepare anything. This took away the dead space in the boxes and made loading them into the food pack easier. Powdered items, like pancake mix or Kool-Aid, were double bagged in case one of the bags tore. In addition to this liberal use of plastic, the food pack itself was lined with a garbage bag. The whole operation was polyethylene overkill, but when it came to food, we figured, "Better dry than hungry." If my friends and I had taken some of these simple precautions on our trip years earlier, we would have had plenty of food and Pete and I would have been able to finish the route. On trips with the brothers, we were all more experienced and wise enough to know it was worth the additional time and expense to waterproof everything.

We never packed much meat because of the need to keep it cold. The two exceptions were beef jerky and smoked, on-the-hide bacon. Paul knew of a good butcher shop on the east side of St. Paul where we could get both products. It was a classic shop with a glass case at the front counter displaying various cuts of meat as well as dried beef products. We typically bought a couple pounds of bacon and beef jerky.

Both of these "gourmet" meats were Paul's suggestion and they were initially met with critical skepticism from Rob, Keith, and me, who were ever watchful of our budgets. It was pricey stuff, especially given our incomes, but after our first taste on that initial trip, all four of us were convinced it was worth every penny. They became staples every year thereafter.

During mornings around the fire, I remember watching Paul cut the bacon right off the pig hide and thinking it was perhaps the strangest way to prepare bacon I'd ever seen. It made the source of our food a bit more real. At the same time, you cannot get meat any fresher or less processed. It was not like the paper-thin, fatty bacon abomination you get in the store. This was "man bacon" that we could cut as thick as we wanted. There was nothing like the thick, hot slices of bacon right off the fire in the morning, grease soaked up with paper towels.

"We'll see if we can't attract a nice big bear with the smell of this bacon," Paul said with a wry grin.

We all gave a nervous chuckle at his attempted morning humor as we sat there, salivating at the sight of the bacon sizzling in the pan. While we'd never encountered a bear in the BWCA, none of us aspired to, either. If anything could lure a bear into camp, it was this, but there were just some things that could not be sacrificed, and hot bacon was one of them.

The jerky was top-sirloin beef, dried, smoked, and seasoned to perfection. It came in flavors like teriyaki and black pepper and was its own source of culinary pleasure for us. Unlike the bland cardboard-thin stuff they sell in bags at the grocery, these sticks were a half inch thick by six inches long. When you started in on one, you knew you'd be busy for a while. It was a marathon for your molars. During some of our portage breaks, everybody would grab a pull and start chewing. You always knew that for the next five minutes or so there wouldn't be much in the way of conversation. There would be an occasional "Mmmm . . . good" or a grunt of some sort, but not much more. Like a gathering of human cows, it was just a lot of cud chewing. It was the kind of meat that made us glad we were carnivores.

Besides the food and equipment, each of us had our own pack for clothes, hygiene items, and personal effects. Like the food packs, these were double lined with plastic garbage bags. This not only kept our clothes dry, but the bags could also be separated later in the trip—one for clean items and one for dirty. The bags served as a vapor barrier to keep the smoke-smelling, dirty garments separate from the clean ones. When you've been in the woods sitting around a fire for a few days, you begin to appreciate the smell of a clean shirt. Smoke, sweat, and dirty socks remind you that vapor barriers are a good thing.

While all of us were fully aware that cotton is not the fabric of choice when camping, we tended to bring what we had. Cotton has a low warmth/weight ratio and takes a long time to dry if it gets wet. None of us could afford GORE-TEX or some of the other high-tech fabrics so popular among camping extremists. Our clothes for the week included a couple pairs of jeans and shorts, a few T-shirts, a couple wool or cotton flannel shirts, underwear, socks, and vinyl rain ponchos.

Footwear for camping, while important, is not as critical as it is in, say, a backpacking trip. As a group of city boys in our twenties, this meant we usually wore sneakers of one variety or another. While Keith and I favored the high-topped leather basketball sneakers, Rob and Brad went for the more traditional cross-trainers. Paul lived, ate, and practically slept in his white Converse All Star High Tops. It was part of his whole punk-rocker persona. Tom, the practical one, elected to make his own stylistic statement in high-cut leather boots.

We were a ragtag bunch. One thing we were not was the clean-shaven fashion models wearing two-hundred-dollar hiking boots and North Face jackets on the cover of Outside magazine.

Once the clothes and toiletries were packed, we were left to decide what else we couldn't do without on the trip. Most of us kept it simple—just the necessities. Paul, however, always managed to bring a few out-of-the-ordinary items. One was his pair of drumsticks. He played drums for a rock band and he liked to practice when the opportunity presented itself. Usually he would set up a life vest on a flat rock near the water on a sunny day and bang out a drum solo or two. While the solitude of the woods was nice, after a couple days the rhythmic drumming broke up the monotony rather nicely.

Another thing he brought regularly was his favorite cassette tape. Even though we never brought a player, he continued to bring his *Clash* tape. He pulled it out of his pack one day and when I asked him about it, he said it was a kind of "desert island" thing. "You never know when you're going to need your favorite tape," he used to say. Oddly enough, we never came across an abandoned tape deck in the deep woods, but if we had, it was good to know he was ready to rock.

After a long night of preliminary packing, we hit the sack to get some sleep. Packing was always the worst part, so it felt good knowing the next couple of days would be easier. They would be spent driving to get the canoes and additional gear at Courage North and then heading to our ultimate destination. Knowing that, soon enough, we would be dipping paddles and casting lines made for a restful night.

The Driving

Getting to the edge of nowhere requires a lot of time behind the windshield or, if you draw the short straw, behind the guy behind the windshield. It requires many long hours watching the white line whiz by. Our rides to the Boundary Waters were usually divided into two parts. The first involved driving about four hours to a facility called Courage North, a camp for kids with disabilities, near Lake George, Minnesota. Rob and Keith both worked there as counselors for a couple summers and, after that, continued on as volunteers to help open and close camp in the spring and the fall. The camp directors were generous and allowed us use of their canoes and other equipment in exchange for Rob's and Keith's ongoing volunteer efforts. It was a great arrangement as we were spared the extra expense of renting equipment every year. We were all on limited budgets, so this provision made the trip much more affordable. Even though this pit stop was many miles out of our way, we were fortunate to have the connection.

The camp itself was quite large and had a number of cabins sprinkled around a central dining commons. From year to year, we stayed in any one of the cabins or in the newly built King Building. King was a beautiful facility with high vaulted ceilings and a welcoming big fireplace surrounded by comfortable furniture. The walls were paneled with knotty pine, giving it an "up north" feel to go along with the sense of new, clean, and modern. The industrial kitchen was impressive as well, with a dizzying amount of stainless steel, lots of cupboard space, and a large dishwasher and stove.

Typically, we drove to Courage North on the first day of the trip and would stay the night. It allowed us to relax after our long ride and to get a fresh start for the BW the next morning. Because the summer camps were done for the year, we had the whole grounds to ourselves. In celebration of being halfway to our destination, we tended to overindulge in beer and bourbon one last time before entering the relative dry zone of the outback woods.

The next day we roused by midmorning and shook off the aftershocks of the previous night's festivities. One by one we emerged from our rooms, worked our way through a hearty breakfast, and started our secondary packing. Packs were stuffed with any Courage North gear we needed and the canoes were trailered or strapped to the cars. When that was done, we started out for the second four-hour leg of our journey. This took us to our BWCA launch point.

*   *   *

One year our trip had a different twist to it, caused in part by our stay at Courage North. The camp had a full-sized gym, mountain bikes, canoes, and every other imaginable outdoor "man toy" you could think of. On the day we arrived, we were suffering from cramped legs and road-weary bodies from being cooped up in the cars. We were anxious to take advantage of the facilities at our disposal in hopes of getting a bit of a workout. We goofed around in the gym for a while, playing basketball and two-on-two volleyball. Later, Paul and Brad took off on the mountain bikes that were available. There were some single-track wooded trails they decided to check out to see if they could squeeze a bit of adrenaline into their day.

During his ride, Paul took some sort of wicked fall and came limping back into camp, holding his back like an old man.

"What happened to you?" I asked.

"Oh, man, this is not good. I really messed up my back on that bike."

"Did you wipe out?"

"Yeah, badly. I've got to go lie down," he said.

He was in serious pain. We told him to take it easy and get rested, and hopefully he'd heal overnight.

The next day, he informed us he was still in considerable pain and couldn't fathom sitting in a car for four hours, let alone paddling a canoe. Because we were all on vacation and had nowhere we really had to be, we tried to take a cool approach.

"No problem, bro. Do whatever it takes to get better. We can hang here another day."

As we said this, lingering in the back of each of our minds was the fear that he would not be better by tomorrow and we might have to shorten the trip considerably or cancel it altogether. We were equally torn by our concern for Paul's well-being and dread that the whole trip might be caving in on us. At the same time, Paul was just as angry at himself for what he'd done. He wanted to be in a canoe as much as any of us. He was a hard worker and sitting still was not his forte, so this was irking him.

He spent the entire day resting and bombarding his system with ibuprofen to help reduce the inflammation in his lower back. Our family has a history of back problems, due in part, I think, to our tall frames. Rob and I were very familiar with the pain he was experiencing. Paul was doing all the right things; we would just have to take it day by day. We filled the time by shooting buckets, playing cards, napping, and trying to make the best of a bad situation.

The next morning, the first question from everyone was, how's Paul?

"I think I can make a go of it," he declared.

"Great! We can help you with your pack or canoes or whatever." Rob offered.

"Sounds good. Now let's get out of this Club Med and get on the road," Paul said with a laugh. We quickly packed our gear into the vehicle and headed north. While Paul was a little stiff and sore over the next couple days, he "toughed it out" and made it through the entire trip.

It gives me pause to consider that, despite the passing of twenty-plus years, the threads that stitched us siblings together only strengthened with time. When the chips are down, we look after our own. If there's one of us in pain, we all feel it. Coming from a big family had its trials growing up, but it never ceases to amaze me to how we step up for one another in times of need.

*   *   *

To say the cars we took over these years were of a higher-quality stock than the Plymouth that Pat and I used years before would be a lie. Most of us were fresh out of college and working our way up, so we usually didn't have a great pool of vehicles from which to choose. The usual round trip covered nearly a thousand miles, so it was important to pick vehicles that appeared to offer glimmers of hope of being able to get us back to our start point.

Our quality criteria were simple. First was the age of the vehicle. Since none of us had a new car, the decision was often a matter of whose was newest. Fewer years typically meant fewer miles, and with that came better odds of an uneventful trip. The only other real criterion was the general running condition of the car. Was it leaking any fluids? Was its exhaust smoke white (antifreeze), blue (oil), or black (Lord help us)? Did it have a spare tire? Was it safe at highway speeds for extended periods? Did it have a tape deck? While a tape deck did not ensure our car would get any farther than one without, at least it could be used to drown out a noisy muffler or other suspect noise. It was true—our dubious vehicle-selection practice added that extra grain of adventure to our already salty trips.

Rob's 1975 Chevy Malibu Classic was the vehicle of choice for our maiden trip of '87. Years earlier, Rob bought the car from our mother when she "upgraded" to a brand new '77 Plymouth Volaré. He needed a vehicle when he went to school in New York, so it seemed like a logical time for Mom to upgrade. In very short order, it became clear that Rob got the better end of the deal. The Volarés and Aspens have to fall among the biggest lemons ever produced at Chrysler. They were forever being recalled or serviced for something.

It was almost like the body and the engine were designed by two different teams of workers who were not in contact with each other. Manufacturing-salary incentives might have been granted for corner cutting, or maybe the company hired engineering flunkies who claimed to be "misunderstood" by the engineering establishment. From the prematurely rusted fenders to the underwhelming slant-six engine to the crackling AM radio knobs, it was all problems all the time for the Volaré. After a series of mechanical problems with the car, Mom admitted she missed her Malibu. By the end of her Volaré experience, she swore to never buy another Chrysler, and thus far she has held to that promise.

The Malibu had well over a hundred thousand miles on the odometer at a time when that was a much bigger milestone than it is today. It was a comfortable big red four-door with cracked vinyl bench seats, whitewall tires, and a throaty V-8 engine. It always had a uniquely pleasant smell to it, thanks in part to the cheap gas-station air freshener Rob liked to hang from the cigarette lighter. It was like a mix of strawberry, women's perfume, and velvet, if velvet had a smell.

It also had the requisite GM fender rust and at least one slightly balding tire. Of course, there were the quirks typical of any high-mileage vehicle—things like sticky door locks, a blinker you had to work manually at times, or a sketchy glove-box latch. The chrome moon hubcaps looked sharp in their own right, except for the one that was missing. The three-hubcap look gave the car just a slight hint of working-class ghetto. Rob preferred to think of these things as "personality." Most car salesmen would call them deductions.

Rob had a habit of naming his cars. The Malibu he named *Christine* after the Stephen King novel, due in part to the car's occasionally temperamental nature. I remember on cold Minnesota winter nights, he would pat the dashboard after a successful start and say something like, "Nice Christine." While I never saw much point in the naming of a vehicle, I had to agree Christine fit pretty well. Whatever it took to get us from here to there was okay by me. That was my take on the whole vehicle-pampering routine.

As big as she was, it was a bit cozy for the four of us—my brothers Rob and Paul and our friend Keith. We brothers were all over 6'3", which meant that whoever got the back seat had to pretzel their way in and out. Because we were all on tight budgets, we decided to make it work. We were not going to let the lack of a better car keep us from our vacation wilderness. Paul, Keith, and I would take turns sitting in the front seat, where legroom was first class, while Rob drove the entire trip. He always said that the time passed faster when you were in the driver's seat. None of us argued with his logic, and it just meant spontaneous naps were ours for the taking.

One of the shortcomings of the Malibu was its lack of a roof rack. Being a four-door, it was clearly a family sedan in an era when that was all a family needed. It certainly wasn't constructed with the thought that strapping two seventeen-foot canoes to its roof would *ever* be a good idea. On the night of the planning, when we realized we'd be taking Rob's rackless car, Paul chuckled and said, "Uh, yeah, we'll figure something out in the morning. I've got some ideas." You never heard that kind of reasoning the night before NASA's space-shuttle launches. This would explain why none of us ended up as rocket scientists, I guess.

The next morning, after a bit of scheming after breakfast, we headed to the logical location to get the materials for our rack—the local Knox Lumber. We ended up buying a couple of two-by-fours in six-foot lengths, which would serve as the canoe supports, and two one-by-fours that would box those supports together in a square fashion. We also bought a box of wood screws to hold the whole thing together.

After measuring the dimensions of the Malibu's roof, we screwed the one-by-fours into the two-by-fours in the shape of a square that would fit on top of the car. Paul made quick work of it with his cordless drill. What we lacked in planning skills, we made up for in construction savvy and ingenuity. When it was done, we stood back and took a look at it. It was a thing of beauty! At a total cost of fifteen dollars, we had ourselves a fully functional, non-DOT-approved canoe rack. Furthermore it was "green" and eco-friendly, so there was that.

We lifted the rack and laid it gently on top of the car. Rob was beyond being concerned about the roof's finish. An underlying blanket would have only served to make the whole deal more unstable than it already was. It sat on the Malibu's roof like a wooden crown of thorns. The rack was then secured to the car by opening the doors and running rope around the column that separates the front door from the back, wrapping it around the rack a few times, and then tightly knotting it. When it was done, the rack's two-by-fours stuck out like dwarf wooden wings on a bad Popular Mechanics aircraft.

After giving the rack a good shake to check stability, we put the canoes on it, one alongside the other. We then used roughly a mile and a half of clothesline to lash them to the rack through the passenger windows. Then we used more rope to put guidelines through the front and rear bumpers. When it was done, it was apparent that while the rest of the car risked falling apart beneath us, the canoes sure weren't going anywhere. I can remember driving through St. Paul on our way to the freeway, looking like four college-grad hillbillies in our urban assault vehicle. It wasn't exactly the immaculate, four-wheel-drive Land Rover you see crossing a mountain stream in the TV ads. Frankly, the only thing missing was Jed Clampett sitting on top of the canoes with his shotgun in his lap.

With the trunk packed to bursting with gear, we set out in high spirits. Fully loaded, the Malibu took on the look of a lowrider as we motored toward our first destination, Courage North. The car's cassette deck served us well. Paul kept it plugged with his choice of the latest alternative band or other artists by request when things got dull. He played everything from the Hoodoo Gurus and the Replacements to Marley and the Dead.

About the only thing we didn't play was the Clash tape, which was safely packed away along with his drumsticks somewhere in the trunk. This didn't stop Paul from spontaneously pounding out the drum parts with his hands on the dashboard or his knees as he felt compelled. Rob always flashed Paul an annoyed grin, but Paul kept pounding away anyway. Surrendering, Rob put the cruise on nine over the limit and we rocked on down the highway. The road was straight, flat, and true and we were on vacation at last!

We breezed along past sleepy central Minnesota farming towns like Avon, Sauk Centre, and Wadena. When we passed through the towns of Motley and Nimrod, we laughed. I wondered how they managed to earn such unfortunate names—names that, despite the town's quaintness or attraction, could never be lived down. Many other towns went by unnoticed by those of us electing to take a nap. Sleep was frequent in the back seat as the front-seat passenger was tasked with talking to Rob to keep him alert. Gas or bathroom breaks were every hour and a half or so and usually involved a small purchase of snacks or soda to keep us going.

Under the monotonous drone of road noise, at the edge of some nameless, unincorporated town somewhere south of Park Rapids, the Malibu began chugging and coughing. It was like the car had air in the gas lines and every time it hit a pocket, it would pop and wheeze for a second. It started slowly, with infrequent occurrences, but steadily got worse until the sputtering moments exceeded the smooth ones.

"Oh, great, how come we had to take my car?" Rob griped.

"Maybe it'll work itself out on its own," I offered, hoping it was a little carbon on the plugs or something benign.

As we chugged along for a few miles, it became apparent the issue was not going to go away on its own, so we began talking about our options. We agreed we should limp it into town and then take a look under the hood. Rob slowed the car to around forty-five and nursed it to the outskirts of the nearest town. We found the first available parking lot and pulled asthmatic Christine in for a look.

Because the two canoes were roped to the top of the car, opening the hood required taking both of them off. We set to the task of undoing the mile and a half of rope with great determination, knowing our vacation clock was ticking. With four of us working on them, it wasn't long before we were easing the canoes off and setting them down in the gravel parking lot.

Paul, being the most mechanically inclined of all of us, popped the hood and surveyed the geriatric Chevy 350 engine. He had one of those inquisitive personalities that loved to tear things apart. Sometimes he would do it to see how something worked, but more often he did it because he thought something wasn't running to his level of satisfaction. This is a trait I neither have nor understand. My philosophy is always, if it ain't broke, thank God, because I wouldn't know where to start to fix it. Paul's penchant for taking things apart drove our mother crazy. Once he spent a princely sum on a new mountain bike and, within a month, it lay in pieces in his bedroom. All she could see, of course, was a broken bike.

"It's got sand in the gear cassette, Mom. I have to do this," he said. Before long though, the bike was back on the road, good as new.

He was the one who would tear apart a toy car and make a helicopter out of it. If it made noise, plugged in, or burned fuel, he needed to know how it worked. He was a deconstructionist—but one capable of reconstruction. This was in direct contrast to me, whose mechanical aptitude was always stifled by the fear that I might disassemble something I could not reassemble. Paul did not know this fear.

He gave the Chevy engine a thorough inspection. He took off the big black air cleaner and checked the carburetor for any blockages or inconsistencies. Next, he checked the tightness of the spark-plug wires and made sure all the belts were in working order. After a few minutes, he came up with dirty hands and his diagnosis.

"It's hard to tell, but I think it might be the distributor cap. That's my guess, anyway." The way the car was sputtering and misfiring, it seemed like a logical answer to the rest of us. Based on his assumption, our plan of action was to continue to limp the car to a service station in town to see if they could fix the cap. Someone needed to stay with the canoes, so Keith and I waited while Rob and Paul went to find a station.

Shortly after they pulled away, I noticed a big liquid stain on the gravel where the car had been. I bent down and rubbed the stain with my fingers. I smelled it and was surprised to find it was gasoline! The problem, it seemed, was not the distributor cap after all. I told Keith that I needed to tell Rob and Paul about it so they wouldn't waste our time and money with a distributor cap. He said he'd stay with the canoes. I took off running in the favored garb of all great long-distance runners: blue jeans, T-shirt, and leather hiking boots. I'm certain the local townies enjoyed it. "Hey, Lorraine, come and check out the city boy runnin' up the highway in his boots!"

After about a quarter-mile run, I arrived at the service station breathless and in a full sweat. When I walked in, Paul and Rob were talking with the mechanic about our options for a distributor cap. I interrupted with, "Guys, it's not the cap. It's something fuel related. There's a big gas stain in the lot back by the canoes." We all went outside to take a closer look at Christine. Paul crawled under the car to find that, indeed, gas was dripping out of the fuel pump.

The mechanic on duty said he was busy with some other work and wouldn't be able to get to us for a few hours, if at all. Things looked grim. At this rate, we would lose almost a whole day if we had to wait. Paul took matters into his own hands and said he could probably do it. With no other apparent options and nothing to lose, we all agreed he should give it a try. Paul borrowed a ratchet and a few assorted wrenches from the mechanic while Rob paid for the pump. As he pulled out his credit card, he uttered the cash-register card salute we always used when we were purchasing something we couldn't really afford.

"Ca-ching!"

"Hey, it's only money, bro." I patted Rob on the back and laughed.

"Yeah, and next year, we'll take your car," he countered. We both laughed and headed back outside. Rob backed the car away from the garage doors to a flat parking area nearby. Paul grabbed the tools and the pump, crawled back under the car, and set to work. Knowing what fueled a good mechanic, Rob and I set off across the street to the liquor store for a case of beer. After our purchase, I grabbed a beer for Keith and walked back the quarter mile to fill him in on the news.

When I got there, he was patiently sitting on the back end of the canoe, perhaps fantasizing he was on a lake and not stranded in some godforsaken parking lot. I passed him the beer. "You look like you could use one of these," I said.

"Thanks, man. What's up?" Keith asked.

"Well, we're looking at a new fuel pump and about an hour for installation."

I filled him in on the specifics and mentioned that I thought we were on the right track. We talked for fifteen minutes, and then I finished my beer and told him I'd go check and see how things were progressing. When I got there, Paul was just finishing his installation. He emerged from under the car with blackened hands and a look of optimism on his face. We passed him a congratulatory beer and asked for his prognosis. "She'll be fine. Fire it up and let's check her for leaks," he said.

Rob climbed in and turned the key. Paul crouched down and checked the pump for any residual gas leaks. "Looks good from here," he assured us.

"Cool, let's go get the canoes and get on the road," Rob said. We jumped in the car and went back to where Keith was waiting. We loaded the canoes onto the top of the econo-rack, restrung the clothesline cat's cradle, and gave a pull to check it for good measure. After the four of us climbed back in the car, Rob pulled onto the highway and wound the engine out. The motor hummed smoothly as the speedometer needle worked its way up through the numbers. Rob patted the dashboard lovingly and said, "Good Christine." We high-fived each other as we knew we were back on the vacation track. To Paul's credit, the pump worked flawlessly for the rest of the trip and for the duration of Christine's lifespan.

The interesting part of the whole situation, though, was how we brothers, including Keith, dealt with an adverse situation as a team.

Everyone knew that sitting idly by and wringing our hands was not going to help anything. We each played a role as individuals in getting the problem solved so life would be better for the whole. Not having a father telling us what to do in tough spots, we relied on each other's direction and advice. We leaned on each other. We'd spent our entire lives doing it—pistons in the family engine, so to speak. And so, when something went awry in our adventures as adults, we just hit the throttle and went to work.

*   *   *

While there were no other major car breakdowns during those trips of the late '80s and early '90s, we always seemed to end up taking at least one motley vehicle every year. One year, it was our friend Brad's 1972 Ford LTD. It was a spacious sedan and, over the course of its lifetime, had become a natural lowrider. Fully loaded, it rode only ten inches from the ground. With heavy, solid doors, a hood the size of a dining-room table, and a sneering big chrome grille, what it lacked in sex appeal it made up for in roominess. It was never our goal to win the auto show with these cars, and Brad's was proof of that.

Another memorable ride was Rob's 1983 Olds Cutlass Supreme. Rob gave this one a name, too, though a somewhat more honorable name this time than Christine. He called it Mary Blue in honor of our mother, Mary Lou. It was a car designed for an upwardly mobile crowd, being a two-door with a fast-back roof and cool opera windows in the backseat. It was a nice, luxury machine in its heyday, but by the time Rob acquired it, it was past its prime. The car had more than its share of expensive repairs under his ownership. Eventually, it began to burn oil rather obviously. I thought it deserved a new name, so I christened it Mary Blue-Smoke.

Rob was not amused.

On the trip of 1989, my 1983 Ford Escort was chosen as one of the two vehicles we'd be driving. This was an eleventh-hour decision driven by the fact that Paul's truck needed a new clutch. When pressed whether he thought it could make it or not, his answer was less than reassuring. Having lived through the on-the-road repair fiasco a couple of years earlier, we decided to go with the lesser of two evils, my car. It meant we would have to pretzel two six-footers into the compact, a bit like clowns in a VW, but we were willing to put up with the inconvenience.

The Escort was Ford's sorely underpowered follow-up to the Pinto. Mine was a two-door hatchback with a 1.6-liter engine and a four-speed manual transmission. If that were not enough, the whole thing was decked out in shoe-polish brown. Yes sir, it was a pimpin' ride. This was a no-frills machine and handled every bit like one. Zero to sixty in a minute and a half, provided you had no passengers and a good tail wind. To call it underwhelming might be giving it undue credit. To call it a wilderness vehicle was an outright lie.

The early Escort models were manufactured with aluminum heads. This design proved to be its greatest weakness, as the heads tended to warp over time because of heat buildup. The only fix for warped heads was replacement at great expense. The telltale symptom of this impending problem was white smoke blowing from the exhaust. This was indicative that antifreeze was leaking into the engine block and being burned and pumped out the tailpipe; never good.

At the time of the trip, my car was in the beginning stages of blowing this white smoke. Knowing this, I hadn't intended on driving it four hundred miles into the wilderness, let alone with a canoe strapped on top. What's more, I had just bought a new Honda and was a week away from taking delivery, with the Escort being my trade-in. The thought of risking the deal by having the car blow a head gasket in Ely, Minnesota, caused me a bit of unease.

However, when faced with the choice between driving the sketchy Ford and not going at all, it was really a no-brainer. I was going to the Boundary Waters if I had to push the car. Nevertheless, before we left, just for good measure, I put a can of STP Gas Treatment into the tank and said, "Tune up in a can. Let's go!" To the credit of the folks at Ford and STP, my car made it up to the woods and back. A week later, I made the trip back to Milwaukee, where I promptly turned it in for my trade. Thank you, Detroit!

While our cars, trailers, and racks were never things of beauty, we always managed to make it up and back. At times, it required tailgating a trailer to prevent the cops from seeing a blown taillight or keeping our speed near the limit for fear of a shifting overhead load. The important thing was the conversations and the quality time spent within the confines of the four-wheeled uglies. Whether it was discussing family dynamics, badmouthing the political hacks of the day, or just rocking out to Jane's Addiction, the point was, we were family and we were together. And we didn't need a Cadillac to appreciate that.

The Resting

On occasion during our long drives, we found it necessary to stop and have a beer in one of the many small towns that dot the northern Minnesota landscape. We usually did this to break up the monotony and, well, because we were on vacation and we could. These were always brief affairs, never more than an hour stop anywhere, but they reenergized our enthusiasm and served as a sort of a team-building session. Heaven knows it's important to build team rapport before spending days in a canoe with someone.

At one memorable stop, Rob, Paul, Keith, and I chose a bar in Park Rapids, Minnesota. Because we were not familiar with the area at all, we just picked a random establishment called the Royal Bar, just off the main highway. We walked in to find a decent-sized tavern with a smattering of locals hunched over the long wooden bar. The air hung heavy with the smell of stale beer and cigarette smoke. Rock and roll thumped from the jukebox and a neon Schmidt beer sign glowed from behind the bar. In the back sat an empty pool table near the restrooms.

Because the three of us brothers all stand over 6'3" and were accompanied by Keith, our African-American friend, we were quickly sized up by most of the patrons. None of us was looking for any trouble, but given the quizzical makeup of our group—three out-of-towners and a black guy—we felt the uninvited gawking of the locals on us like a bad case of poison ivy. There just aren't a lot of blacks this far north of the Twin Cities and, as much as you try to ignore it, sometimes skin color is difficult to overlook.

I turned to Keith and said in a low voice, "Feeling a little out of place?"

Keith had been in that kind of situation before, so he just laughed. "Yeah, it's cool, though." His personality is so laid back that he's hard to rattle.

I'm not sure how Rob and Paul felt about the stares and glares we were getting, but it certainly unnerved me. You see, our father, Roy, was murdered by four African-Americans in a bar fight in St. Paul in 1967. The bar was located in a racially sensitive neighborhood during one of the more racially tense periods in America. My understanding is they beat him up, fled, and then returned a short while later and beat him again, fracturing his skull. It was an allegedly random act of violence—a case of being in the wrong place at the wrong time. None of those circumstances makes what happened right, but based on the undue attention Keith was getting in this bar, the situation we found ourselves in was becoming downright eerie.

We ordered a pitcher of beer at the bar and ambled back toward the pool table. All of us were capable players, and nothing is more relaxing than a game of pool with friends while enjoying a beer. We paired up and played a game between ourselves. During the game, a couple of the locals put a pair of quarters on the rail of the pool table, signaling a challenge to the winner. While we would have preferred to keep the game and table to ourselves, we weren't going to back down from a challenge. Rob and Paul ended up winning and thus faced off with the locals.

Being the winners, Paul broke and the game started. It was a back and forth affair. Team Landwehr sunk a couple, and then the locals countered with a run of their own. During the game, one of the players had a bad case of "oral diarrhea" and did a fair amount of smack talking. He took the liberty of commenting on how weak the break was and how it left both teams with tough shots. After that, he made a point of snickering at their misses, to the delight of his teammate. He was an extremely unlikable person who effused arrogance. His voice was the kind you could hear across the bar and had difficulty tuning out. It was clear he frequented this bar as he knew the bartender and a few of the patrons. His brash character was backed up by his big, flashy wristwatch. Annoyed by the guy, Paul quickly tagged him "Rolex Boy."

Because of their hearing loss, Rob and Keith couldn't hear much of his nonstop chatter, but Paul and I did. I'm much better at letting that kind of thing roll off my back than Paul is. He has a more reactive temper, and it was starting to show. He returned to the area where Keith and I sat and muttered something about how Rolex Boy was starting to bug him. I agreed, but I told him to stay cool. This guy was clearly not worth wrecking a good vacation.

Eventually, Rob and Paul lost the match. Rolex Boy gloated at what was no doubt the high point of his day. Rob and Paul, using their best barroom courtesies, said, "Good game," and returned to the table with Keith and me to help finish the pitcher. Paul continued to express his contempt for Rolex Boy and his running commentary. We filled Rob and Keith in on some of what was said, and they both agreed the guy was a loudmouth.

With the pitcher drained and with no reason to stick around and listen to this guy's irritating monologue, which continued at the bar, we decided to get back on the road. We sauntered out of the bar into the afternoon sun. As we walked toward the car, Paul said to me, "Hey, Jim, did you notice the bar sign back there?"

"No, what about it?" I asked.

"The bar sign. The A in ROYAL was burned out. The 'ROY L,' get it? And three of the Landwehr brothers were just there."

"Wow. That is kinda freaky," I said, and I went on to tell Rob of our strange revelation. He too was unnerved by the irony of the whole circumstance.

Now, I'm not sure if I can articulate the significance of this sequence of events.

First of all, there was the whole black/white thing, only in reverse this time. We could sense the unease of the bar ratchet up a notch when we walked in. Heads turned and craned. People tend to notice when a black man walks into a lily-white bar in a predominantly white, backwoods town. And try as they might to appear unaffected, it was clear there were some people not comfortable with Keith's presence. Fortunately, no racial slurs were uttered, at least that we could hear. If there were, I'm certain Keith would have been defended by all three of us. We are quiet guys who keep to ourselves—unless provoked. Then, all bets are off.

Then there was Paul's near-miss exchange with Rolex Boy and his volcanic jawing. Unfortunately, I never knew my dad well enough to see what his temperament was like or to know if it played a role in that fateful night in '67. However, I did know Paul's temper could be explosive at times and I was glad to see him take the high road and contain himself.

And finally, there was the burned out letter A. The fact that, of all the bars, in all the towns in the state, we walked into the ROY L. What are the chances? One in a million is my guess. If it had been the Y or the O, the entire event would probably have been forgotten and it would have been just another roadside bar in another town on another trip.

It's my belief that it *was* fate, somehow just meant to be. Perhaps we happened upon that place for some predestined reason. Maybe it was to show us the wretched ugliness of racism and how, despite being twenty years after our father's murder and the race riots of the sixties, we still had a long way to go. Having Keith in our midst made us all keenly aware of the stares and glares of racism not only here but in places back in the cities as well.

Or maybe we were just called to that place for the sake of appreciating the gift of our brotherhood and reflecting on our father. Elements of his character were likely in each of us, though we'd never had the chance to see which of our traits they were. I have a handful of memories, but Rob and Paul have nothing but pictures and family lore to help them understand him. Furthermore, if you asked each of his six living children to tell the story of his death, we would probably give six different accounts. It just wasn't talked about much. As a result, we were left to look at each other with our strengths and differences and try to formulate our own picture of who he was.

We climbed into the car, two in front, two in back. We slowly worked our way back through town to the main highway and continued our trek northward. None of us talked much about the weird coincidences. I can't help but think, though, that at points during the rest of the ride and perhaps the rest of the trip, each of us worked through the significance of us all being together at that place.

Together in spirit with Roy L. at the ROY L.

The Launching

As mentioned earlier, our departure points were usually one of two locations: Snowbank Lake or Mudro Lake. The launch at Snowbank Lake was well maintained with ample parking, a sign post with maps and regulations, and a trash dumpster. It's one of the few lakes on the fringe of the BWCA that actually allowed small-motored boats. Because of this, the boat landing was made to accommodate trailers and had a gently sloped drive with long parallel timbers leading into the lake. While departures from this entry point always went off without a hitch, there was one particular launch from Mudro Lake that was not quite so forgettable.

The easiest access to Mudro Lake was by parking in a lot on Cedar Lake Road, a half-hour drive out of Ely. This lot was also the location of the last tavern between Minnesota and the Canadian border. Known by its catchy name, the Chainsaw Sisters' Saloon, the place was named after its two burly female proprietors who had, at one time, worked for the US Forest Service. The sisters charged a small daily fee for allowing a vehicle to be parked in their lot and then keeping an eye on it. It's now defunct, but at the time, this tavern, like many others in Minnesota known as three-two joints, served only beer and wine. The three-two label comes from the maximum-allowable alcohol percentage in the beer. In this case, 3.2 percent was all it took to fuel the devastation that was about to unfold.

Out front, a large round sign hung from the blade of a huge chainsaw held up by a pair of pine logs with a cross brace. A weathered set of stairs fashioned out of timbers led up a sloping hill to the front entrance. The saloon was an unassuming small wooden building with a large open-air porch, great for a relaxing smoke or a game of cards.

Inside was a long bar with eight or nine high-backed bar stools as well as a few round tables. A small tape player and radio sat on a window ledge next to a shelf full of cassettes comprising the low-budget jukebox. A big dog charged with keeping the peace slept on the porch. On the floor against the far wall sat a huge decommissioned chainsaw, giving the patrons a feel for the hard life of a modern-day lumberjack. A couple of cheap wildlife prints hung in frames on either end of the bar. On this occasion, streamers and balloons were strung from the ceiling in celebration of Labor Day.

Tacked on the wall behind the bar was a T-shirt with the Chainsaw Sisters' logo. The back of the shirts had their slogan emblazoned on it: "I got buzzed at the Chainsaw Sisters' Saloon." The ceiling was covered with dollar bills with owners' names and trip dates written on them. We each bought a T-shirt and then added to the ceiling fund with a dollar of our own, scrawled with "The Landwehr Brothers and Friends" on it. I sometimes wonder where that dollar bill ended up.

The year of this particular trip, the saloon was running a Labor Day special. For a five-dollar cup, you'd get all the beer you could drink. Yee Hah! As young, rambunctious voyageurs on a budget, we stumbled into an oasis beyond any we could have dreamed up. Of course, it doesn't take a risk-management professional to pair a bottomless beer cup with a canoe and come up with a bad scenario, any way you slice it. Suddenly, the T-shirt slogan took on new relevance.

At the tavern, there was much drinking of cheap beer, backslapping, and card playing. We rejoiced in our brotherhood and the fact that we were creating a canoeing tradition our father would have been proud of. In some respects, it was through this kind of fellowship that we connected with the man none of us had ever really known. By getting to know each other better in an environment he loved and had visited himself, maybe we could begin to understand what made him tick. We each had questions about him, and by working alongside each other through the week, maybe flashes of our own character would provide some answers. I don't think it was ever a conscious intent, but none of us could deny ruminating on what he might think of us being together in this place.

Around six o'clock, after a few hours of adult-grade nonsense at the saloon, we decided we should get moving toward our destination. After all, we still had about a mile to paddle downstream, which would take us to Mudro Lake. The lake had a number of sites on it, and we hoped to make one ours for the night.

We said our goodbyes to the sisters, which included them indulging in a photo op and T-shirt signing, and headed out into the waning afternoon sun. Paul and I were canoe mates in one boat, Rob and Keith in the other. Those two teamed up well, as they were both hard of hearing. They could sign back and forth as needed and didn't need to rely on lip reading. Paul and I both knew enough sign language to get the point across but figured they would have an easier time of it with each other. He and I worked pretty well in a canoe, too. That's not to say there weren't moments when he or I *wished* we were hard of hearing. It would have eliminated the need to listen to gripes about the other's paddling technique.

When we arrived at the parking area a few hours earlier in the day, we unloaded our canoes into a small creek on the upstream side of a bridge that passed through the launch to the bar parking lot. Tired and lazy after a long day of warming a stool at the bar, we decided it was easier to just put in and duck at the low bridge rather than move the canoes and contents to the other side. It looked moronically simple, especially given the confidence a full afternoon of drinking provided. Piece of cake.

Rob and Keith climbed in their canoe and managed to maneuver themselves under the bridge with a bit of man-giggling but without event. Now it was our turn. I hopped in the bow and Paul took the stern. In an effort to maintain our balance and unerringly pass under the low bridge, Paul said something like, "You lean back and left, and I'll lean back and right." Or maybe it was vice versa. Because we were both wearing "beering aids," our inability to properly hear, register, or, evidently, tell our left from right was the source of our impending ruin.

What transpired next is still a source of debate. Somewhere, about halfway under the bridge, the canoe began a barrel roll to the right. Evidently, we *both* leaned back and to the right and we were suddenly in what is known as naval distress, with a heavy list to starboard.

It couldn't have been more than a second or two when we both realized what was happening and tried to correct our error. Unfortunately, our canoe was like one of those dippy drinking birds with the red water in them. Once it reaches a point, there's no stopping it; weight and gravity win out. We plunged into the cool water beneath the bridge. When we surfaced, arms flailing, we shouted commands to one another and thrashed about. Not surprisingly, we also achieved instant sobriety. It was not our finest hour.

Daddy would be so proud.

After guiding the submerged canoe under the bridge, we dragged it over to the nearest bank. The two of us slogged to shore, much to the amusement of Rob and Keith, who were enjoying the synchronized drowning routine from the cheap seats of their canoe.

"Nice work, boys." Rob laughed. "You guys okay?"

"Yeah, we're fine. Just a little canoe issue," I said.

"Canoe issue? More like a sailor issue," Rob countered.

"Ha ha. I wonder if anyone in the tavern saw that whole escapade," I said.

"I hope not," Paul replied with a laugh.

The two of us collected ourselves and attempted to contain the debris field. Because much of our gear was in large Duluth packs, most of it managed to stay wedged in the canoe underneath the thwarts and yoke (the curved center bar that holds the pads for carrying the canoe overhead). As in any disaster, we looked to the high-priced items first. The tents and sleeping bags were all accounted for, so we had that much going for us.

My heart sank when I realized the biggest hit I personally took was my 35 mm SLR camera. I unzipped my camera bag, inspected it, and found the camera had water somewhere in between the viewfinder and the lens. I spent the next two weeks trying various techniques to get the moisture out. Eventually I was successful and, while the pictures from that trip were lost, the camera actually worked for a few years after. The ironic thing was that, earlier in the day, Rob offered to store my camera in his waterproof bag, but I turned him down. "It'll be fine," I said. Fine indeed.

There were other unsecured items that met a watery grave, including fishing rods, my tackle box, and a few undocumented objects. Many of these are likely still on the river bottom, awaiting Robert Ballard's dive team and serving as breeding grounds for walleye and bass.

Paul and I wrung out our shirts and took stock of the damage. Outside of my camera getting wet, we were most troubled by the loss of our fishing rods. They were our main source of recreation during the week, and no rods meant no fish. After we determined they were the biggest loss, we spent a couple of minutes rehashing the whole experience with Keith and Rob. They were still in a state of hilarious disbelief. "Shut up and let's go so we can get a fire started and get out of these wet clothes," I said. We climbed back in and started on the way to our site.

The paddle down the stream toward Mudro Lake took close to an hour. Because darkness was setting in fast, as we paddled we schemed that we could camp on a small nearby island we knew about from a previous trip. When we arrived at the lake, however, the island was occupied by another party. We were forced to resort to plan C. I'd like to say this was a well-thought-out backup to the backup plan, but it was more along the lines of spontaneous improvisation.

We paddled to the nearest shoreline of the lake and surveyed the situation. By this time it was twilight, and our accommodation options were few. We found a small clearing along the shore and paddled to it. When we arrived, we saw the remnants of a campfire and staked the makeshift site as ours for the night. Other than the campfire pit, this site had nothing going for it. It was sloped and rocky but, frankly, it was our only real option at the time. Wet beggars can't be choosers.

The canoes were pulled up the embankment and unloaded. Paul and I changed out of our wet clothes and we all gathered and took a walk around the uncharted site. Because of its small size, the steep pitch of the ground, and the fact that much of it was rock, we were unable to set up any tents. After surveying the situation, Paul said, "Guess we're sleeping under the stars."

"Yep, kinda looks that way," I agreed.

Paul and I hung as much wet equipment as we could on the surrounding trees. The evening air was starting to get rather cool, so we gathered up some wood and got a fire started. Paul cooked a light dinner, and we talked and joked for a while and decided to make it an early evening. We laid down our quarter-inch foam sleeping pads on the rocky dirt, unrolled our bags, and wriggled in. I cinched my mummy bag around my head so only my nose and mouth were exposed.

It was a restless night for all of us. Over the course of the night, the pitch of the ground caused us all to slide slowly down the embankment toward the lake. Every hour or so we would wake and inch our way back up the incline like oversized caterpillars. Sleeping under the stars lakeside is, well, not like you see in the movies.

None of us got much sleep. Paul fared the worst. His sleeping bag got pretty wet during the canoe baptism, so he ended up sleeping in a dry change of clothes with only an old wool army blanket to shield him from the cool night air and his thin pad to smooth out the rocks and roots. The rest of us slept on our pads on top of our warm, three-season sleeping bags on the uneven embankment. I'm sure it looked like a great northern refugee camp. The next morning we shared how each of us slept.

"I think I got about three good hours of sleep," I said.

Rob and Keith nodded their agreement.

"Man, I slept horribly. I was freezing! If I got two hours, I'd be surprised. I wanted to drag that smoldering cedar log into my blanket," Paul said. He took one for the team for sure.

After a simple breakfast, we regrouped and decided that most of what was lost was expendable, with the exception of the fishing rods. Those we wanted back. We decided to return to the bridge for an underwater salvage operation. We figured if we could recover either of the two rods from the river bottom, the operation would be considered a success.

We loaded the equipment back into the canoes and headed toward the stream. After an hour of paddling upstream, we arrived at the scene of the previous day's disaster. Like any good marine archeological dig, we did a site assessment and surmised that, yes sir, the rods were likely right under the bridge.

I would put the stream under the bridge to around five feet deep, so getting to the bottom would be a challenge. Paul, bound and determined to get his rod back, assumed the role of diver. He took a big breath of air and dove down for his first attempt. His legs kicked and thrashed at the top of the water as he fought the current and foraged on the bottom for any signs of his rod. After ten seconds or so, he came to the surface empty-handed and breathing hard. His failure only spurred his motivation, so he took another breath and dove in, and the flailing and thrashing continued. Again he came up with nothing.

On his third dive attempt, he managed to surface with a fishing rod. I secretly hoped it was mine, but it turned out to be Paul's. You'd have thought he found a full bottle of champagne from the Titanic. We all cheered, knowing our chances at a fish dinner just increased substantially. We encouraged him as he made a couple more futile attempts to retrieve the second rod or any other artifacts. When he had enough and was tired, he came ashore and dried off. Overall, it was a commendable effort, given the stream depth and current. For a brief moment, we deliberated about having a celebratory beer at the bar but reasoned we had better declare victory and move on before anyone recognized us from the day before.

And so the lore of the famed "Chainsaw Launch" lives on. The canoe-tipping event, while a breach of all good canoeing practices, actually could have been much worse. Unlike the senior-class trip I took some years before, we prepared for that very scenario by waterproofing all of our food and clothing and therefore came away relatively unscathed. Furthermore, it was these kinds of hysterical, lifelong memories that kept us coming back year after year.

The Paddling

Canoeing, reduced to its simplest elements, is really just the execution of controlled chaos. It consists of a series of coordinated, contradictory movements by two people, meant to advance the whole in a positive direction. It's a bit like a good marriage, really.

In a perfect scenario, each person paddles from opposite sides at precisely the same time with exactly the same effort. The two opposing forces then move the craft in a straight line and the result is one hundred percent efficiency. In reality, what usually happens is the person in the stern starts to criticize the bowman's technique and effort. They then feel compelled to offer unsolicited advice to the bowman on how to improve one or both. This leads to the bowman feeling underappreciated and so the sniping begins. It can make for a caustic mix.

As brothers, we got along pretty well while canoeing in the Boundary Waters. Historically, this was not always the case. We've been getting together in boats in pursuit of fish for many years, and our relationships were not always amicable.

On one occasion in the early '70s, our family rented a cabin in Forest Lake, Minnesota, a short thirty-minute drive from the Twin Cities. Like all good resorts, it was comprised of six or seven cabins on the lake and had enough activities to keep us occupied all day. Rob, twelve at the time, and Paul, a year younger, decided they were going fishing. Because they were close in age and size, it theoretically seemed like a good match. After Mom instructed them to stay within sight of the dock, they each grabbed an oar, strapped on a life vest, and started rowing.

After a short time, the performance complaints started rolling in. Because sound carries so well over water, we, and the rest of the resort, heard many of them.

"Row harder," one said.

"*You* row harder," the other countered

"We're going crooked, you idiot!"

"You're doing it wrong, you de-horn."

To this day, I don't know what a de-horn is, but it sure makes a great insult. I think its origin can be traced to Tom, though I'm not sure he'd care to own up to it.

The scenario was like Laurel and Hardy at the lake; *Babes in Boatland*. All that was missing was the squeaky music and bowler hats. The irony is that the scene was a foreshadowing of some of those canoe matchups many years later. As we grew up, technical-correction advice and outright insults were still hurled, just at a more civilized volume.

In fact, antagonistic paddling criticism was an affliction that crossed the generations rather nicely in our family. My dad and his brother once competed as a team in a multiday race from Bemidji to St. Cloud, Minnesota. The story goes that Dad climbed out after a long first day of paddling and arguing and said, "I'm done! I can't paddle with him anymore." Mom said that after spending the night away from his brother, Dad eventually came to his senses and did return the next day. It turns out they both channeled their frustration into their paddling and their canoe ended up taking second place in the race. He was just a victim of that well-known affliction I like to call "canoe clash."

Over the course of our years together in the Boundary Waters, reactions like my father's were completely understandable. We fought with our canoe mates periodically in the course of every trip, at least in our minds if not verbally. Put-downs and ridicule usually spurred one's partner into elevating his game, once he mopped up his self-esteem from the floor of the canoe.

"Paddle harder, you wuss."

"Hey, your skirt's dragging in the water!"

"No, your other left, you de-horn!"

"What, are you sleeping back there?"

These outbursts were all part of our contribution to the magnificent wilderness experience. Which insult you dialed up was dependent on the situation, but it was best to be well versed in *all* of them. Besides, it helped blow off some steam and shatter the serenity. We wouldn't want too much of that, would we?

*   *   *

The weather in the Boundary Waters often determined how far we could paddle in a day. We always kept a watchful eye on the skies, and while heavy rain tended to force us to hunker down until it passed, we did do our share of paddling in light drizzle in order to make a distance goal.

Because our annual trip occurred post–Labor Day, the daytime temperatures were not usually an issue. The cool night air, on the other hand, sometimes served to drive people to the warmth of their tents in spite of an inviting fire. Often after a long day of paddling and fishing, a warm tent sounded better than enduring a cold night, sitting on a log and trying to coax a blaze.

Wind was always unwelcome but usually only presented a problem when we were on some of the larger lakes and whitecaps started to form. On one trip, in 1988, we were forced to sit tight for a day and a half while steady ten- to fifteen-mile-per-hour winds battered us. This set us back from our scheduled pace but was the safe alternative to the risk of paddling in whitecaps. Canoeing in that kind of wind is not only extremely hard work, it's dangerous. The waves get large, frothy, and menacing and can come at the canoe from a number of directions, increasing exponentially the risk of swamping. Sitting in the wind is a drag, but it beats bobbing in the lake by a long shot.

By midmorning of the second day, the wind subsided to the point where there were no whitecaps, but it was still blowing pretty hard. We were at a crossroads, and rather than continue to sit, we decided to harness the wind's power for good and use it to our advantage. In our quest to make up some lost time and save a little energy, an idea was hatched. We would rig up a sail spanning the two canoes which would power us across the lake in record time. It was clear that, like Columbus and other explorers before us, we had too much time on our hands.

The design team set to work. Using some rope, we tied the two canoes together at the thwarts. Then, in order to achieve maximum sail area, the spare stern paddles were lashed to the outside of the forward thwart of the canoes using worn bungee cords. To make the sail, a heavy-duty vinyl tarp was pulled between the two stern paddles and wrapped tightly around them, and duct tape was placed along the seam. It began to take on that Huckleberry Finn appearance.

The navigation and steerage system consisted of two paddles being used as rudders at the rear of the craft by the highly skilled helmsmen, Rob and Paul, in this case. Unfortunately, their view was essentially blocked by our sail, a design flaw I'd prefer not to take credit for. This meant that Keith and I were left to the front seats to guide them in the direction of our portage landing.

When it was finished, it was a wickedly decrepit-looking watercraft; a kind of twentieth-century _Kon-Tiki_. I liken it to the Corvair, a car made famous for its design flaws in Ralph Nader's book, *Unsafe at Any Speed*. This was a bit like the nautical equivalent, unsafe at any depth.

As we shoved off and began our journey on our untested, maritime dice roll, we found the wind was in our favor and we covered the first hundred yards or so in relatively good time. We were sailing and life was good! As we got further into the open water, however, our clever plan began to founder. The craft's numerous design flaws started appearing like a bad rash. Its biggest shortcoming was the sheer mass of the vessel. The combination of gear and passenger weight made it heavy and difficult to steer. It handled like a runaway barge. Add to this the fact that it was a rectangle and, well, you get the idea. The best we could hope for was to try to keep some semblance of a straight course toward the shore we were hoping to land on.

Keith and I attempted to help keep our line, but our efforts were largely in vain. Because they were the only decent source of steerage, Rob and Paul quickly became the whipping boys for our mystical line of travel and seemingly random course adjustments. "Right, right, right!" I shouted.

"We're doing our best," Paul replied from the rear of the craft.

"Are you guys hitting the Jack Daniels back there?" Keith added.

"Keith, it's not as easy as it looks to control this thing," Rob said defensively.

There's nothing like the support of a good crew when things start taking a turn for the worse.

After about a twenty-minute sail, the wind that had been our nemesis for so long gradually came to an end. We began to drift slowly and aimlessly, like Ty-D-Bol men in our aluminum dinghy. We came to a quick consensus to abandon the plan and cut our losses before we lost any more time. The sail was dismantled and all hands resumed their normal posts. Keith and I grabbed our paddles and the four of us finished guiding our fledgling craft across the lake. Like many of our adventures together, it wasn't perfection, but it sure turned an ordinary day into an unforgettable one.

*   *   *

Paddling and camping with a group is great fun on days when everything is clicking. If the weather cooperates, waters are calm, and everyone's emotions are in sync, there's nothing better than slicing through the lakes and streams with the sun on your face. The anticipation of the unknown up ahead sprinkled with the fellowship of the brotherhood and friends makes for light, worry-free travel. It's when things aren't going so well that the group dynamics make good fodder for psychological study. Personalities come to the surface in the face of adversity and it can be a little like reality TV without the cameras.

In 1991, our party of six planned to save some time by taking a shortcut down a small stream shown on the map. On paper, it seemed like a great idea. We were soon to discover there are real-world things you cannot plan for when looking at a dated, two-dimensional map.

Once we found the inlet, we paddled in. The stream was about fifteen feet wide and a few feet deep. It felt a little unnerving to be off of our originally intended course, but that is a key element of any adventure—the thrill of the unknown. We recognized that and forged ahead into this unknown with confident trepidation. After about ten minutes on the winding, muddy-bottomed stream, it suddenly became much wider, eventually ending in a pond. It became clear that the pond was the result of a monstrous beaver dam. We worked our canoes up to the dam and climbed out to survey it. It stood probably thirty inches above the water line and, at twenty feet across, it was quite a structure. It was testament to the term, "Busy as a beaver."

We decided to cross the impediment using the carry-over method. This involved leaving the equipment in the canoe and each team of two taking opposing ends of it. From there they would count to three and heft it across the dam using muscle and brawn. We cursed under our breath as we lifted the heavy canoes, baby-stepped over the beaver dam, and set down on the other side. It was a lazy man's portage and a positively vertebrae-compressing way to move a boat.

After all the canoes were across, we climbed back in and continued down the stream. A few minutes later, we started scraping bottom. It seems the beaver dam took the rage out of the river and we were beginning to experience the effect of the low water. Before long, all three canoes were at a complete stop. The reeds and marsh grasses on both sides of the stream seemed to close in on us. They were tall and thick, and even when we stood up in the canoe, we couldn't see far enough to find our outlet into the next lake.

Being men, our first course of action was to try brute strength. We pushed and poled with our paddles to no avail. After some failed attempts to power-paddle our way out, everyone just kind of stopped and sat there, looking at one another. We were literally bogged down in a bog. We couldn't really get out of the canoes without risk of sinking up to our waists in muck.

We hadn't reached complete panic mode at this point, just a sort of dumbfounded shock state. After a minute of talking about what to do, Rob noticed the slick blackness of a large leech attached to his paddle.

"Oh, great, look at this."

"Ah, ha ha ha!" Paul laughed.

He then reminded us all of the scene from *The African Queen* where Humphrey Bogart was pulling the boat through the marsh only to find he was covered in leeches when he got out of the water. Even strong, cool Bogie was a bundle of nerves after that. After recounting it a nervous laughter rippled through our party. It would take a boatload of modern-day Kate Hepburns to get any of us into that water, that much we all knew.

Given the dire situation we were in, various personality quirks began to surface. Everyone deals with adversity differently, and this was a classic case study. If this had been a reality show, we would have begun voting people out of the canoes based on their reactions to the circumstances.

I will refrain from using names or trying to categorize any specific people, but there were essentially three types of personalities that came to the surface. First off, there were the Worriers. These folks, once they realized the full extent of our peril, determined that the best plan of attack would be a controlled meltdown. This group's solution consisted of imagining the worst and asking, "What are we going to do?" None of us had the answer, of course, but it was pretty clear that trying to worry the problem away wasn't going to solve anything.

The second group fell under the title of the Inactives. These guys believed that if they thought about it hard enough or waited long enough, maybe the water would rise on its own and float us to safety. Their solution was about as effective as the Worriers, but if we were left under their command, we might still be there in the clutches of that stream's muddy bottom.

The last group was the Desperadoes. Fueled by a blend of panic, action, and adrenaline, these types thought that muscle and raw strength were all the skills necessary to solve their dilemma. It was the Bruce Willis *Die Hard* approach. ("You're messin' with the wrong guy!") It wasn't always completely effective, but no one was going to slight them for their effort. The muscles kicked in about the time the brains shut off.

After watching each other manifest this temporary insanity for a bit, everyone took a breath and came back to their senses. Based on the earlier leech incident, it was clear to everyone that getting out into the muddy river to pull us out using a rope was an absolute *last* resort.

Eventually one of the canoe teams determined that using a coordinated effort of synchronized seat rocking, paddle poling, and cursing, they could inch the canoes forward a bit at a time. Some found it helpful to count out "1 – 2 – 3" and then lurch their bodies forward in tandem, trying to will some momentum out of their canoe. Others took a more freestyle, random approach. It was quite a scene; six grown men lurching and jerking forward in canoes, moving at a snail's pace in the suction cup river.

After about ten minutes of doing the canoe herky-jerk, we finally freed ourselves from the clutches of the murky river bottom. The entire escapade was a test of will, teamwork, and determination. Despite our differences in opinion and methods, we literally pushed on and got through the ordeal together.

Shortly after we wrested ourselves free, we paddled a bit and came to the lake at the end of the muddy river. About fifty yards off shore, Paul and our friend John pulled their canoe up to a large, nearly flat rock. The rock was an attention-grabbing sight in that it rose up out of rather deep water. The glaciers had done great work on this area thousands of years ago and left things like this all over the place in their wake.

Paul got out of the canoe, in part to scout the lay of the land and in part to lay some sort of claim to the rock, like William Bradford did at Plymouth. He stood on the slick, flat rock, tall and lanky in his white Converse high-tops, black jeans, and denim jacket, looking speculatively over the horizon. It was a portrait of punk rocker meets Pere Marquette.

"What are you doing, Paul?" Rob inquired.

"Making a plan up here," Paul replied, pointing to his temple.

The rest of us laughed as we knew it was more about the curiosity of the rock and a chance to stretch his legs than any sort of plan being devised.

At just that moment, without warning, Paul slipped on the flat basaltic rock and went down hard on his back. *Thwack!* It was like the sound of meat hitting a slaughterhouse floor—an unmistakably organic sound that resonated pain and suffering in both the maker and his audience. As he writhed for a couple of seconds, his legs extended into the cool water from his feet up to his knees.

"Ooooowwwww!" Paul shouted.

The rest of us reacted as most people do when someone takes a clownishly tragic fall of any sort. We all laughed for just a few seconds at the sheer stupidity of his fall, but then, when we realized the potential gravity of the situation, we inquired, with smirks on our faces, "Are you okay?"

"Uh, yeah. Owie. Rock's a little slippery," Paul said with a grin, embarrassed by the pratfall.

When it was clear that he was okay, the real gut-level laughter started for all five of us spectators. His falling was one of those scenes that replay in your mind over and over after they happen, each time bringing a slightly more contained laugh. Paul took off his high-top sneakers and wrung out his wet socks. After a minute or two of working through the residual pain, he stood up, collected his dignity, and piled back into the canoe. Luckily, he wasn't seriously hurt. Considering our stressful situation a few minutes before, his mishap actually lightened everyone's mood again and served as a great fireside story for the rest of the trip.

One of the coolest things about our trips to the Boundary Waters was that none of us was exempt from a moment of humility and subsequent ridicule for our acts of stupidity or gracelessness. We all cared deeply for each other and would do anything for the other if the need arose. But as men in the woods, we also operated under the principle that if you couldn't take a little razzing or derision at times, then you should stay at home. We were all up there to laugh and have fun, and sometimes that meant that *you* were the source of the entertainment, like it or not.

*   *   *

I am known in the family as the sibling most likely to die in a drowning accident. I love the water but have pretty weak swimming skills. This makes for a dangerous mix. I was the one who never wanted to go out to the diving raft when our family went to the beach. The water at the dock was always over my head and I was unsure I could swim out that far. As a result, I usually hung out with the younger kids and stuck to where I could touch bottom.

With the exception of the incident with my high school buddies in the rapids disaster of '79, I never had any near-death drowning experiences in the BWCA. However, on the 1990 trip I did have a particularly bad twenty-four-hour period where my lack of canoe-entry finesse created a couple of embarrassing situations.

The first occurred when the four of us brothers and our friends Keith and Brad were scouting what turned out to be an abandoned portage. Everyone except Brad and I landed and were standing around, trying to surmise if it was indeed the portage we were looking for. Brad and I eased alongside the other boats as the canoe bottom bumped against a deep large rock on shore.

I was in the bow of the boat and, thus, first to get out. I stepped my right foot onto the landing and climbed out of the boat. When I placed my left foot onto the large rock, it slipped on the algae and I started to slowly slide down into the water. Before I could compensate to correct it, my other foot followed suit and began to slide too. Gradually I sank as I slipped down the rock until I was submerged up to my neck. It was a slow, steady progression with me gaping at my brothers in disbelief. They were in no position to prevent the dunking, being doubled over with laughter. All I could manage to utter was, "Aaarrrggghhh!!!"

Eventually, Rob lent me a hand and helped me out of the lake. I climbed ashore, took off my shirt, and wrung it out as best I could.

"Jim, if you wanted to swim, you probably should've changed into your swimsuit," Tom joked. Acts of stupidity, accidental or not, were not granted much mercy around camp.

It made for a long afternoon of paddling in a T-shirt and jeans that clung to me like a second skin. To make matters worse, jeans dry extremely slowly in the cool northern air. When we eventually found a campsite, I immediately changed and hung my wet clothes on a line to dry. Luckily, I had a second pair of jeans to wear while that pair dried out.

The following morning, I woke early as I heard Tom taking one of the canoes out for an early-morning fish. After he pushed out, I got dressed and crawled out of my tent, thinking I'd get some fishing in myself. I loaded my rod and tackle box into one of the two remaining canoes and started out.

Typically when I'm getting into a canoe, there is already someone in the back, or stern, who serves to steady the boat. My technique involves pushing them out in the boat until I can no longer stand on dry ground. At this point, I give one last push and kneel gently on the bow until the boat is freed from the shore. Then I complete the maneuver by slowly turning and sitting on my seat. When properly executed, it is an exercise in grace, balance, and, I'll admit, a bit of showmanship.

It seems that during my solo voyage, I forgot to take into account the seventh rule of aquadynamics: *Balance − Mass = Instability*. It's a little-known rule but, as I was about to learn, an important one.

I was excited at the thought of getting some fishing time alone — just me, the loons, and hopefully a couple nice walleye. I lifted the front end and gently eased the canoe into the water, being careful to be quiet so as to not wake any of the other four guys. At the water's edge, I gave my final push and knelt on the bow, thinking I would walk my way back to the rear of the canoe once I was in it. As I knelt on the bow, the almost-empty canoe began to roll to the left. I frantically tried to counter the roll by leaning to the right, but instead experienced the eighth rule of aquadynamics: *Imbalance + Panic = Chaos*.

The canoe continued its roll until it was free of its human burden. The thoughts going through my head were, *Oh no, gonna get a wet boot. Ooops, wet pant leg. Argh, I'm going in!*

Sensing my impending doom, I tried to minimize the noise of my entry so as not to disturb those who were still sleeping. It seemed the selfless thing to do. Some would argue that I did this to avoid the embarrassment of being caught in the act of a self-inflicted drowning, but I'm sticking with my original claim.

My attempts to muffle my failed launch were successful. Neither Tom, across the lake, nor any of the other four guys heard or witnessed my debacle. I bobbed around in the water, up to my neck again, groping for the edge of the canoe. I quietly did the breaststroke back to where I could stand and slogged onto shore like the Creature from the Black Lagoon, dragging my defiant, wicked, evil canoe behind me. I pulled it up to shore, careful not to bang the bottom and wake anybody. The last thing I needed was to provide more fodder for those in camp who had already witnessed the lakeside baptism less than twenty-four hours prior. I slogged up to camp, soaked and completely humiliated.

I quickly found my pack and changed into dry clothes. I had more than enough shirts, but at the rate I was dunking them, dry jeans were becoming a bit of a premium. I wrung out my jeans and shirt, rolled them up, and put them in a garbage bag at the bottom of my pack, hiding them like a kid who just wet the bed. I changed into my pants from the day before that were still a bit damp. Within an hour, the rest of the crew started waking up and crawling from their tents. "Good morning," I said, trying to act nonchalant and not tip them off to my mishap of a few minutes prior. I must have done a pretty good cover job, as no one ever found out about this second embarrassing event—until now, I guess.

The Portaging

Part of the beauty of the Boundary Waters is that in the more remote areas, you can paddle for days without seeing another soul. Getting to those areas requires portaging between water bodies. This involves transporting your boat and gear across short, and sometimes not so short, stretches of land. The terrain, trail conditions, and how well you packed often determine your experience. For the most part, though, it is not for whiners or slackers. Having participated in enough portages, I've drafted my own definition of portaging you *won't* find in Webster's dictionary, and it goes as follows:

Portaging (pōr-tij-ing)

1. A voluntary death march across godforsaken terrain in the name of transporting a boat from one body of water to another exceedingly similar body of water.

2. A self-inflicted hardship involving backbreaking labor, often producing random hallucinations and coarse language.

It is hard, sweaty, thankless work.

The portaging experience begins with you and your canoe buddy deciding who gets to hoist the canoe overhead and carry it to the other side. Because we usually went three or four portages deep on each trip, we alternated who would take the canoe and who would take the packs and other gear.

The process of loading the canoe ranged from a thing of beauty and grace to one of an Olympic sport gone bad. The canoe hauler began his hoist by centering himself on one side of the canoe, where the shoulder-padded yoke was. He grabbed the yoke at the opposite side from where he stood, took a deep breath, and lifted the canoe so that the gunwale nearest to him rested on his thighs. From there, using a turn and a bench-press motion, he lifted the yoke over his head and set the pads on his shoulders. This sometimes resulted in the stern or bow banging on the ground as the handler struggled for control. What was intended as a one-two-three motion often turned into a four-five-need-some-help-here-six motion. Eventually, though, liftoff was achieved and the canoe-bearing Sherpa began his trek.

While loading the canoe on our shoulders was always a treat, walking the actual portage trail was when the real fun began. It wasn't so bad when we were moving the canoe across those short, flat, straight stretches we rarely encountered. It was those hilly, rocky portages strewn with ankle-turning roots that made us question our use of vacation time. Portages that we swore were cut by drunken, practical-joking Forest Service employees, designed to weed out the weak and uncommitted.

Some of the longer portages even had two or three canoe "rests" along their length. These were locations where some merciful worker fashioned an overhead hook where people could set the canoe to regain the feeling in their shoulders and perhaps receive CPR or stress counseling. There were a couple of these rests where, by the time we got to them, we were seeing visions of the Virgin Mary, Jerry Garcia, and Elvis. Trails like these were life changing.

Hilly portages required a great deal of strength, grace, and balance. A third lung helped, too. Walking uphill or downhill with a sixteen-foot aluminum teeter-totter on your shoulders is not for clods or the weak. Occasionally, as we descended a hill, we forgot to watch our stern, and the back end would bang on the rocky trail. If you were the second or third canoe in a train, you just followed the noise in front of you and traveled by sound alone, kind of like portage foghorns or audible GPS. It also tipped you off as to where to lift your back end so as to not look as inept as the guy making all the noise in front of you.

There's an unspoken understanding among the portaging brotherhood that whoever's wearing the canoe is King of the Trail. If you're packing anything less, yield or suffer the righteous tongue-lashing of the guy with the canoe. When you're carrying the canoe, your field of vision consists of your boots and about ten feet in front of them. At this point, you're a visually-impaired, oxygen-sucking, one-man right-of-way.

Over the years, we took to naming some of our portages, much like they name tropical storms and with the same degree of humility and respect. For instance, there was "Swamp Portage." It was a low-lying pathway cut through the forest where, if we diverged from the main path on either side, we were bound to get our feet wet. In some areas there were logs laid down in the dirt to enable campers to traverse an unusually damp section. It was a tricky trail even without the burden of packs or a canoe. It was here that Keith discovered the law of physics that dictates, *When humans are burdened with large watercraft overhead, essentially all balance and equilibrium is negated by said craft.*

Rob, Paul, and I had dropped off our packs at the end of Swamp Portage and were sitting on large rocks, waiting for Keith to come with the last canoe. Being shorter than the three of us, he always had a tougher time with portaging and this time was no exception. Eventually, he came lumbering along, breathing hard and trying to stay on the slippery narrow trail. As he mimicked parkour down the trail, suddenly his sneakered foot slipped on a rock and the momentum of the canoe overhead took control. The weight combined with the sudden shift in balance steered him off the path and into the shallows of the duckweed swamp.

"Aaawwww, man!" he groaned as he sloshed through the muck in his high-top sneakers, trying desperately to correct his course.

"Taking a shortcut, Keith?" Rob asked. I'm not sure, but I think Keith actually freed one of his hands at this point to give Rob a universal sign-language answer to his question in his own meaningful way. We all laughed as Keith squished his way to the end of the portage and performed his canoe dismount. We could laugh at his debacle because we all knew too well that it could have just as easily been any one of us in his place.

*   *   *

Regardless of the footwear we chose, one of the more vivid memories was spending most of every trip with one wet foot. The methods by which the shoe got wet varied, but the actual process, for me, at least, was cyclical until the trip was over. The most frequent source of wet feet was the canoe launching. The canoes are often pushed off into the lake amid a field of seemingly benign boulders and faux stepping stones. While some of these rocks are flat, dry, and secure, many of them only appear so at the surface. When stepped on, these ankle benders always catch the stepper off guard. Usually they're resting on a rounded rock beneath them that serves as a fulcrum for what quickly becomes a teeter-totter rock.

These misstep adventures are favorites of mine when I am the spectator. There's nothing like watching a companion's shoed foot slide down a deceivingly flat rock right into the water and then listening to the curses resonating off the lake. These mishaps always get a good group laugh started. Of course, courtesy dictates that you ask the person if they're okay after you're done guffawing. It's the polite thing to do.

There are a number of other ways to inadvertently get a wet shoe. Certainly any activity undertaken "down by the canoes" is a direct invitation. Activities like doing the dishes, fishing from shore, and filling the water containers are all prime candidates. Another sure thing is the ever-tantalizing downed tree extending into the water. There is some sort of dangerous allure and almost a spellbinding pull that forces us against our better judgment to see if we can traverse these makeshift bridges as a means to an end for tasks like freeing a lure or exiting a canoe. It's as if putting on hiking boots somehow makes us as deft as one of the Wallendas. The outcome is rarely favorable as gravity and inept balancing usually win out.

On most trips, no sooner did one foot dry than the other ended up getting wet through some misstep. It was incredibly frustrating. After a day spent drying out a shoe, you began thinking you were finally in the clear and then, *sploosh*, and it was time to start the drying process all over again. Having one wet and one dry foot created not only discomfort for the rest of the day but also a strange sense of imbalance. It's a little like having one shoe tied tighter than the other—not a showstopper, but one of those irritations you just kind of roll with in the great north woods.

* * *

Hoary Portage, so named by Paul, took its name from the word "hoary" we discovered on the label on the back of a bottle of Yukon Jack, a Canadian whiskey. The label read: "Yukon Jack is a taste born of hoary nights when lonely men struggled to keep their fires lit and their cabins warm." In recognition of our proximity to the great country of Canada, we usually brought a canteen of it for those moments requiring an attitude adjustment. The name Hoary carries no reference to the actual portage characteristics; we just liked the word.

Typically when we got to a portage, we would each load up with equipment and start off down the trail and walk at our own pace. Because of the timing, there were cases when we would get separated by a minute or two on the trail. In this particular instance, all of us except Paul made it to the end of the portage and we spent several minutes waiting for him. Paul got seriously sidetracked while taking a wrong turn on one of the deceptive forks along the path.

"Man, what's taking him so long?" Rob asked.

"I don't know, maybe we should go back and see if we can find him," I said.

"He'll figure it out eventually," Rob assured us.

Shortly after Rob's display of grave concern, Paul emerged, bearing bug bites and branch scratches from his unintended diversion. He explained that he got disoriented and wandered down the wrong path. After backtracking for a bit, he began to panic to the point that he said he was thrashing through the underbrush. After some anxious moments, he eventually located the main trail and found his way to us. After listening to his adventure into uncharted wilderness, there was an undercurrent of chortling among all of us, Paul included. Again, once we realized he was safe, we could all enjoy a laugh at his expense. It was his hoary experience.

* * *

On a portage on the trip of '88, I managed to lose my glasses. I like to refer to this as "Fuzzy Portage," as that sums up what I saw for most of it. I only needed the glasses for seeing distance, so I kept them in an easy-to-reach pocket of my camera bag. They were put there because, when it wasn't accidentally being dipped in the lake during capsize, the camera bag was one of the few portaged items that garnered some respect. Most other items were treated with the care typically given airline baggage. Knowing the specs were tucked away, I figured they would be fine.

Because I didn't need the glasses for the grueling portaging process, I tended to put them in the camera bag during the crossings. On this particular occasion, it was after a second long portage that my glasses were missing from the case. I determined that I must have lost them two portages prior to where we were. When I broke the news to the brothers and Keith, they were several shades short of compassionate. Hard, grueling work carried us this far, and to backtrack at this point to look for a needle in a haystack was not an option. Being tired, I had to agree.

"Sucks to be you," I think someone said at the time. I was feeling the love. Not *seeing* it so much, but definitely feeling it.

I only have mild nearsightedness, so it just meant that everything distant looked soft and fuzzy. The scenic beauty of the Boundary Waters is held in its magnificent vista, best enjoyed when you can see them clearly more than twenty yards ahead of you. In a pinch, squinting works, but over time it gets annoying to the ones you're with. They took turns squinting back at me to remind me what I looked like.

A couple of days passed and we were working our way back out through the same route we entered. As we came to the beginning of the hellacious portage, I saw that some Good Samaritan had found my glasses and placed them on a large boulder.

"Alleluia," I yelled as I put them on. "I can see!"

It was wonderful to again be able to see the beautiful details of nature that had become hazy for the past couple days. Birch trees and their glorious white bark skin jumped back to life for me. Felled trees lying in the water regained their clarity. Eagles soaring overhead could be seen in detail. It is amazing what you don't realize you have lost until you find it again. All of this thanks to a conscientious fellow camper who took the time to help a stranger.

*   *   *

A couple of other portages just fell under the broad name of Widow Makin' Portage. It was the name we gave to any portage that taxed us to the point of great discomfort. It could be bugs, terrain, length, or all three combined that earned these trails their moniker. While we didn't relish these difficult portages, we all understood that, in order to get to the remote campsites and the promise of solitude and more plentiful fish, they were part of the whole experience.

The Fishing

Though all of us claimed to be accomplished fishermen, our record in the BWCA was, let's just say, less than amazing. It was not for lack of trying, though some years we focused on fishing more than others. In the end, we always seemed to have an ample supply of excuses: too late in the summer, too hot, too cool, tidal pull, solar flares. You name it, we used it. In our case, "accomplished fishermen" really meant that we'd never lost anyone at sea.

This is not to say we didn't catch any fish. It's just that our day jobs were never in jeopardy. When we did catch fish, most were average in size. We caught northern pike, bass, and an occasional walleye. All were of good eating size but were no real trophies. There was, however, the mother of all fish stories in Paul's battle with the much-heralded "monster" walleye.

Near dusk one evening, we were paired up in two canoes—Paul and Rob in one and Keith and me in another. It was one of those perfect evenings for being on the water. The air was warm and windless, creating a mirror-like surface on the lake. The lonesome, whippering call of the loon occasionally rang out to remind us that we were mere visitors in this hallowed place. It shaped up to be the kind of night I wanted to blister into my memory to be recalled when work became stressful or when life crashed around me.

I don't remember which lake we were on, but that's irrelevant anyway, given the fisherman's number-one rule:

Never disclose the actual location of where you caught your fish.

The premise is, if you are asked or approached about details, keep all your answers vague on locations, weather conditions, bait, and depth. If pressed for details, you are permitted to call on the second rule of fishing:

When asked for specifics by potential fishing-spot parasites, lying is not only permissible, but encouraged.

Adherence to these two commandments leads to answers like, "Yeah, we were kinda in a shallow bay with deep drop-offs on the leeward side of one of the islands on the northeasterly part of that big lake, I forget the name, just outside of Ely about ten or fifty miles. We were using natural bait and some lures about halfway between the boat and the bottom. It was partly cloudy with some rain and sun at times."

These descriptions will throw them off the scent and they won't likely ask again.

So, on the unnamed lake so many years ago, Paul began hooting and carrying on, yelling for Keith and me to bring the net. Because we never had great luck fishing, we brought only one net for two boats, thinking that would be plenty. Fisherman's luck would have it that the boat without the net always gets the biggest fish. You can almost guarantee it.

"Hurry up, this fish is pulling the canoe around!" Paul yelled. Based on the urgency in his voice and his play-by-play description, Paul was in the process of landing Moby Dick. Rob calmly helped maneuver the canoe with his paddle while Paul fought the great fish.

Keith and I, excited that anyone had a fish on his line, quickly reeled in our own lines, picked up our paddles, and began to work our way frantically toward their boat about two hundred yards from us. As we approached, I got the net ready while Keith continued paddling. When I reached to grab it, I noticed that my lure was snarled in it. In my haste to paddle over and deliver it to them, I had set the lure directly onto the net webbing.

"Argh! Would you look at this? What the . . . " I complained as I struggled with untangling the treble hooks.

"Hurry up, this fish is barely hooked!" Paul said, reminding us all that it was the fish of a lifetime.

Realize that getting hooks out of a net under relaxed "normal" conditions requires a great deal of patience and fine motor skills, a bit like threading a needle. Conducting it in the rear of a surging canoe with adrenaline racing through your veins and the requisite hook-in-finger sticks added a tragically humorous bent to the unfolding drama. All that was missing was Curly, Moe, and an eye poke.

After a few minutes of paddling, Keith and I arrived with the newly freed net to find that, sure enough, there was a fine looking, twenty-seven-plus-inch walleye floating on its side next to the canoe, resting from its long fight. We passed the net to Paul—neither Keith nor I wanted to be responsible if something went awry with our landing technique. As Paul carefully dipped the net in, the fish sensed his destiny and, with a flap of his tail, flipped off the hook and swam free into the crystal-clear water. Paul slammed the net into the water with a vengeance and proceeded to utter a litany of profanities that killed a few small birds in the area. He was fuming mad.

As fellow fishermen, we felt for Paul. At that young age in our lives, big fish were hard to come by, so no one liked to miss a beauty like that one. He claimed that all he wanted was a picture of it and seemed to find little comfort in the fact that at least we all saw it. As fishermen, we are called to "boat the fish"; anything less is like getting a spare in bowling. It's good but incomplete. Paul stewed about it most of the night and on various occasions throughout the rest of the trip. It's one of those stories that are still the source of great fireside conversation on the rare occasion when the brothers are all gathered.

*   *   *

One of a fisherman's most feared disasters is equipment failure. No one wants to be the one whose reel self-destructs in the middle of catching a fish, forcing them to pull in the fish manually, hand over hand. I've done that on more than one occasion and can confess that the fish is at a distinct advantage in that situation. The other disaster in fishing is the dreaded broken rod. Whether it gets slammed in a car door, gets stepped on inadvertently, or just decides to break midcast, it pretty much ruins your whole day.

Rob fell victim to this experience on one particular trip. Because the lakes in the area have such rocky bottoms and are littered with downed birch and pine trees, snagging lures is commonplace during fishing ventures. Couple the obstructions with our most commonly used lure, the Rapala, a minnow replica that has three treble hooks on it, and you have a recipe for inevitable disappointment. The trick is to try to limit the disappointment to losing a six-dollar lure and not a thirty-dollar rod.

One afternoon Rob managed to get hung up on a particularly stubborn snag while fishing with Keith. He tried all the usual tricks. He started by getting right over the top of the lure and yanking. No joy. Next, he tried the old bow-and-arrow release trick, where you pull the line tight, then grab a section near the reel, stretch it back like you're drawing a bow, and then let it snap. The sudden change in tension will sometimes shake the lure loose. This was not one of those times. The lure was hung up on the bottom, and hung up good.

Well, drastic times called for drastic measures. Determined not to lose another six-dollar lure, Rob resorted to the fisherman's last recourse. This involved whipping your fishing rod back and forth maniacally while testing your recall of four-letter profanities. It was the fishing equivalent of a bigger hammer. Saner moments might bring a person to cut the line and take the loss. That is also a fisherman's admission of defeat and is to be avoided at any cost.

In the middle of one of his finer whips, we heard the dreaded *snap*! Rob stood there, dumbstruck, with half a shattered rod in his hand. "Oh no! Damn it! You've got to be kidding me! I was hardly pulling it." Paul and I laughed mightily, showing our best sibling compassion at his loss. We did it in part because we both knew it could have very easily been one of us on the splintered end of the deal.

"Looks like you're Keith's fishing guide for now," I said with a smirk.

"Very funny, Jim," Rob said unamused.

Later that day, back at our campsite, he set to work to try to repair his rod. The damage was fairly extensive, but he was patient and meticulous. His tools—one pocket knife, four inches of duct tape, a little heat from the fire, and a liberal dose of prayer. He trimmed the shattered shaft away with the knife and then held the smaller portion over the fire to soften the fiberglass. Then, he inserted the piece into the hollow of the larger piece and warmed the entire new joint over the open flame, hoping the heat would serve as a bonding agent between the two. Next, he affixed the oversized duct-tape Band-Aid over the top of the joined pieces.

After an hour or so, he was finished. It was not much to look at but would have to do. He gave it a few good shakes and a couple of us commended him on his handiwork. All of us, including Rob, knew that if it were to be tested with a sizeable fish, it likely would serve only to disappoint. It would allow him to wet a line again tomorrow, though, so it would have to do.

The next day, he managed to get his line hung up on another rock on a different lake. Knowing the strength of the rod was compromised anyway, he worked the snag with a little less zeal than the day before. Despite his attempts to not repeat his fate, he snapped the rod again. There are reports that his angry, profanity-laced response was heard in parts of suburban Ely later that day. He seethed.

I believe all subsequent trips included a backup rod in Rob's canoe.

* * *

Historically, we usually caught enough fish to make at least one fish dinner. These meals were always extremely gratifying. Not only was the fresh fish second to none, but the satisfaction that came out of knowing that we caught it made it even more enjoyable. It was usually breaded in corn meal and fried in either residual bacon fat from breakfast or vegetable oil. Served alongside pan-fried potatoes, it made for a hearty, filling dinner.

In order to get to the frying pan, the fish needed cleaning. Each of us brought a different aptitude for this to the table. Tom was the most proficient at it, in part because he tended to fish more than the rest of us. Paul was decent at it as well. Rob and I were willing to take on the task but were a bit more hackish in our methods. It was really just a matter of experience. Personally, I'm not a big fan of filleting fish, and it typically shows when I'm done with my butchering. I end up with bone-filled fillets that look as though they were cut with a crossbow or maybe a hammer. It's the reason I don't hunt. That would mean I'd have to pluck and butcher a bird that I don't much like the taste of in the first place. For this reason, I'm big on the idea of catch and release.

Personal differences in fish-cleaning techniques took a turn for the worse on the trip of '87. Rob landed a nice northern pike that we all agreed would be our dinner that night. We pulled into our campsite and, after unloading the canoes, Rob set to work cleaning the fish. He took the big pike off the stringer and went over to a large flat rock to begin his project. He started by cutting behind the gill and then back toward the tail.

Now, a word of advice is in order here. Cleaning fish is best done in the company of either someone less willing than, or at least as forgiving as, yourself. If there is any perceived level of competitiveness between the cleaners, nothing good can come of it. If that same competitiveness goes back twenty-plus years in family history, the fish would be better off flung back into the lake in the name of keeping the peace.

As Rob dragged the knife along the midsection of the fish, Paul offered some corrective advice on how to avoid getting the Y bones in the fillet. It was late in the trip, and tempers were starting to get a little short. When you're with siblings for more than a few days, years of "junk" tends to rise to the surface. Rob appeared a bit agitated at Paul's unsolicited advice, but he was determined to prove his capabilities. He said, "Paul, it's my fish, I'll do it." Nevertheless, he took note and continued on. After a few more seconds, Paul again interrupted and said, "You're cutting too close to the spine. You're gonna get all those Y bones in there."

"What? Fine, you do it!" Rob stabbed the fillet knife into the wide-eyed fish head and walked off in a huff.

Keith, Paul, and I looked at each other with astonishment. As we stood there, awkwardly looking at the sorry, knife-impaled fish head, Paul tried to plead his case to Keith and me, but we needed no explanation. We had watched it all transpire and saw both sides of it. Paul's advice may have been correct, but that was not the issue when it came right down to it. The fact of the matter was that Rob had caught it and, like it or not, he would clean it. Eventually, after a few tense moments around camp, Rob cooled off and returned to finish cleaning the fish and the two made their peace.

The whole episode was really about the culmination of four days of too much togetherness smashed against twenty-plus years of family dynamics. As brothers, no matter how we tried to ignore it, there was always a level of competitiveness between us. At this age, we had all been out on our own a while and were busy trying to forge our separate identities. When thrust back together for days on end, we tended to fall back into old familial habits of criticism, nitpicking, and one-upmanship. There were not many run-ins like this over the five years we took trips together, but the whole episode was a reminder of the reason people leave their families in the first place to begin their new lives.

*   *   *

Our friend Keith was never much of a fisherman. He always fished along with us and seemed to enjoy it, for the most part, but never quite shared the success we did. What may have been his biggest catch, a catch none of us will ever forget, took place under the cover of dark one night.

As we gathered around the hearth and started our dinner preparations, Keith decided that rather than waste a perfectly good, dead sucker minnow, he'd try to get some use out of it. He wandered down to the waterline and got his rod out of the canoe. He reached into the bucket and grabbed one of the few remaining minnows. They were much less elusive when they were all floating on the top with those unmistakably clouded dead-fish eyes. He strung the slimy corpse onto his large hook and then reared back and heaved the rig into the water just off shore. To keep the fish from dragging it into the water, he propped up the rod with some large rocks at the base. The bobber sat on the dark water and, after watching it for a few seconds, Keith returned to the fire to relax with the rest of us.

After dinner and the dishes were done, we all gathered around the fire for some chat time and a bit of card playing. Periodically Keith used a flashlight to check his bobber on the dark lake. After an hour he lost sight of it, so he jumped up and, with his flashlight, stumbled down to check his line. From the water's edge we heard him shout, "Hey, I've got something! It's big, too!" We all scrambled to the shoreline to watch Keith fight his fish, hoping his luck had changed and he would land a nice one.

When we arrived, Keith's fishing rod was bent in a wicked arc. He reeled in what little line the beast would relinquish to him, periodically surrendering some line as the fish made a run. "Play him, Keith. Play him. Let him take it," Rob said. A fish dinner was always at the back of our minds and so we all hoped his advice would help Keith finish the deal.

Keith battled for about ten minutes. As his catch neared shore, it became obvious that this was no ordinary fish. In fact, it was not even in the fish family. When we first saw the black shell of what turned out to be a large snapping turtle, we all busted out laughing, including Keith, who could hardly believe his misfortune. Here he pictured a trophy walleye and bragging rights for future years and ended up with Tommy Turtle.

It was unclear who was more upset with the encounter—us or the turtle. With the aid of a couple of flashlights, we could see the turtle's long, sharp claws as he pushed off on the rocky shore in full reverse. The turtle was hooked in its upper lip and was justifiably pissed off. We could see the pink of his mouth and his gnarly turtle tongue as he hissed at us. I always thought turtles were silent creatures, but this one had a definite opinion and was readily voicing it.

The other thing this turtle brought to shore with him was a serious stink. It smelled like a combination of swamp rot and dirty diaper. The odor rolled off him every time his shell broke the surface of the water. "That thing stinks!" Paul shouted. The turtle's eau-de-muck came from living its life on the bottom of the lake and was a reminder to us where it should return.

After we had enough gawking and amusement with Keith's prehistoric amphibian, we decided to free it. Because of his threatening demeanor and smell, no one wanted to try to take the hook out of his lip. The easiest way to deal with the problem would be to cut the line. Rob quickly whipped out a pocketknife and cut the line about a foot from the turtle's mouth. It was as close to the hook as he dared to go. The turtle, sensing his release, turned and kicked his way back into the lake, sporting his new lip bling and consequent monofilament leash.

We all turned and congratulated Keith on the catch of the day. Keith took it in stride, as he did with most everything. He always had a smile to offer, and this was no different. He knew that while he didn't land the trophy fish he hoped for, he would have a story that would be just as memorable. Besides, bad fishing action was better than no fishing action. "Hey, at least I didn't get skunked today," he said. We all had to agree that he was right about that.

* * *

Fishing continues to be part of the glue that holds us brothers together. In 2004, Rob organized a guided fishing trip up to Mille Lacs Lake in central Minnesota, and though the fishing was less than spectacular, it was still a great chance to spend some time on the water with each other. It was filled with the usual teasing and trash talking, but there was a fair amount of backslapping and bonding as well. In fact, one of the unexpected perks of this trip was a snapshot of all four of us at the dock holding our catches. It's one of those iconic pictures that will likely turn up in family-history compilations generations from now.

It's an interesting picture because, for most of us, the only memories we have of our dad are the photos we've seen. In some of those, he's shown in a canoe or holding a fish. It wouldn't take much of a stretch of the imagination to see him set in the middle of this picture, holding his own fish. I do know that if he were still around, there would be no place he'd rather be. In the end, I think it was his influence on Tom and, subsequently, Tom's influence on us brothers that instilled a love of fishing in all of us.

The Camping

Because a campsite is a temporary home for a day or more on your trip, you really want to find a good one. While some of the smaller Boundary Waters lakes had three or four sites, larger lakes could have ten or more. Since we never knew how many other canoeists would be camping for the night, finding a free site could be a real challenge at times. Finding a quality campsite with good loading access, a decent vista, and an abundance of firewood was even more difficult.

There were many forgettable sites for us over the years as well as a few gems. The good ones usually had some unexpected appeal that made them stand out from the rest. Sometimes, this took the form of a nice large rock outcrop jutting into the water that would allow us to sit and enjoy the sunset, filet our fish, or just hang out. Often, we would sit on our life vests on the rocks, reading the tabloids or napping in the sun while Paul pounded out his own private drum solo on a nearby pack or vest. He never traveled very far without his drumsticks.

Sometimes we found a site desirable because someone left a rig in place for hanging a food pack or maybe because it had two or three decent spots for tents. The first would save us the work of finding two suitable trees to hang the food between, and the other meant that there would be no arguments over whose tent went where.

A "good site" was always a relative term that depended on the happenings of the day. Each morning we'd usually measure and plan roughly where we thought our distance goal should be. Then, after paddling to that lake and scouting a few sites, we'd choose the best. On days in which we paddled in a drizzle or it was getting late, we tended to settle for sites that were less than perfect. In some cases, that meant anything with a fire grate and a toilet.

Setting up camp was always done with efficiency and purpose. Usually it was toward the end of the day and, since no one wanted to do it in the dark, our first order of business was getting the tents set up. The favored tent of our particular group was the Eureka two-man Timberline model. It was an A-frame tent that was easy to assemble, lightweight, incredibly durable, and effective at shedding water. Near as I can tell, there was really only one drawback to these tents. During their assembly, they required two long strings to be stretched from the rainfly and staked into the ground on either side of the tent. These guy lines pulled the rainfly taut and helped it to serve as a roof to the tent.

What the tent instructions didn't point out was that these lines create a series of trip wires that become invisible to the naked eye after dusk. Someone tripping over one of them in the night was as predictable as someone walking through the sliding screen door at the family deck party. It was especially entertaining when the victim was walking with a cup of hot coffee or cocoa. We all did it at some point, each man trying to come out of it with a sense of dignity. If you were really good, you could make it look like you'd done it intentionally in kind of a spontaneous camp dance move. More often, though, you ended up doing a cartoonish pratfall for the enjoyment of the rest of the camp. Your best hope was to stick the landing and end up on two feet.

*   *   *

Once our temporary domiciles were constructed, we turned our focus to food. Dinnertime was approached with both a sense of joy and dread. A long day of canoeing worked up big appetites. A hot meal was the perfect answer to hunger pangs after a day spent burning serious calories. Snacking on granola, trail mix, and beef jerky during our paddle was fine for lunch, but when dinner rolled around, we wanted something hot. As much as we looked forward to it, dinner was a mixed blessing for us because we all knew the effort necessary to prepare the meal—forage for firewood, get some water from the middle of the lake for cooking, boil the water, prepare the meal, and worst of all, wash the dishes.

The makeup of all of our meals was usually carbs to restore what we burned during the day's travels. I recall lots of pita bread, macaroni and cheese, and fried potatoes, all made better with a squirt of fake butter or a splash of powdered milk. The potatoes, in particular, were always a burden because of their weight. We made it a point to eat them on the first couple nights of the trip to reduce our load early on. They were delicious and filled any void the main course might have missed.

Paul was, by far, the best cook. He always tried to spice things up with whatever was available, usually bacon fat or some flavor-blasting spice he brought. Because cooking duties were spread out over the whole group, the rest of us resorted to staying within the confines of whatever packaged item we were cooking that night. Delicacies such as ramen noodles and Rice-A-Roni were common entrees. We saved the boxed au gratin potatoes for those evenings when we were feeling cultured.

While most meals were unremarkable, one comes to mind as unforgettable. Being tired from a long day's paddle, we got a late start preparing dinner. While I forget what the main course was supposed to be, one of the side dishes was baked beans. As we prepared the beans in a billy pot on an open fire, we watched the lightning approaching on the horizon. "Think that's a storm coming?" Rob asked.

I answered, "Nah, it's just heat lightning, I think."

"It's so cool to watch," someone else added. We watched with no real sense of urgency, as there was no wind or thunder.

Then what I remember as the telltale drop occurred. You know the sort—a rain drop that hits the dirt with a thud and leaves a divot. Before any of us had time to think, *boy, that was a really big drop*, a few more hit. Then the sky suddenly opened up and it was raining buckets.

Welcome to bedlam.

The camp took on the scene of an ant colony after the anthill had been stepped on. Every ant-man had a role at the point of disaster, and rank and status meant nothing. We scurried around, bumping into each other and trying to minimize the damage and fix the problem.

"Cover the food pack!" someone ordered.

"Close the tent doors!" countered someone else.

"Where's my flashlight?" came another unanswered plea.

The focus was very clear at the time; get anything of value under a tarp or into the tents. Everyone scrambled around, taking care of their own stuff at the speed of light. It was the quickest any of us moved the entire trip.

Once things were covered, the focus of the entire group shifted to priority two: hot beans! The four of us gathered under a tarp around the pot of baked beans. Knowing that we probably would not see a main course that night, we each grabbed a spoon and dug in. It was clearly a case of the fastest eaters getting the biggest take, so we scarfed with abandon. We ate every last bean as we stood in the driving rain with the tarp propped up on our heads. By the end, we were all hunched over the empty pot, not full, but momentarily sated. It was a sad sight, really—very paleolithic man.

But those beans were the best I've ever had.

*   *   *

After our meals came dishwashing, a job we always dreaded. The process required crouching down on some flat rock during the wash, rinse, and dry process. The black soot that coated all the cookware used on the open fire made dish duty a dirty, unrewarding job. The soot stuck to your hands and was dissolvable only by gasoline or paint thinner, it seemed. The stuff got on everything—clothes, packs, Brillo pads, you name it. I think I still have some under my nails to this day.

I compare dealing with the soot to a time, as a young father, I was changing my daughter's diaper. At one point, I found that my shirtsleeve had dragged in the "poo." I didn't see it until it had spread to my arm and then my wrist, and it seemed like every time I looked it was on another part of me. It was not a good feeling. It was almost as if it were multiplying on its own somehow. Mutating, jumping poo! The soot was a lot like this. Careful as you were, it always managed to soil something in the area. By week's end, most of the cookware had areas of soot that were beyond help given the environment we were in. We usually dealt with the issue when we got back home and had access to hot running water and clean scrub pads. There are some things only the modern niceties of life can remedy.

*   *   *

The afternoon sun slowed the fishing action enough that lunch, naps, and an impromptu game of Hacky Sack became our preferred activities around camp. Hacky Sack is one of those strange pseudo sports that surfaced in the '80s. It was largely played by teens and twenty-somethings and consisted of players forming a circle and trying to keep a beanbag airborne between them using anything but their hands. As I recall, Paul pulled one out of his backpack the first year we went up, and for years thereafter, it kind of became one of those silly traditions that you looked forward to, in an odd sort of way.

Unlike accomplished Hacky Sack players, a typical Hacky Sack "rally" in our group was about three kicks. Each kick was usually less controlled than the previous one. This typically meant that the third one would be a desperate, lunging boot that would send the sack hurtling well outside the circle, followed by the two nearest it contorting their legs into unflattering positions in a failed attempt to keep the rally alive.

With most of our group being tall fellows, I'm sure this was a sight to behold from the vantage point of passing canoeists or from any vantage point, for that matter. Four grown men were twitching and flailing their legs and feet, all in the quest to keep a beanbag from hitting the ground. Couple this with the fact that one or more of us usually ended up playing it in hiking boots and, well, I'm guessing the voyageurs never saw such a spectacle. Indeed it may have been, but to us, it was a great way to pass the time, have some laughs, and get a little workout in.

* * *

Some of the more annoying creatures around camp were the chipmunks and red squirrels. The red squirrels, particularly, had a noisy raucous titter that often woke us up in the morning. Both of these animals spent much of their time on the perimeter of our camps, constantly on the lookout for open packs or dropped food. Some were bold enough to enter camp while we were present and forage through our food pack if it was left unattended. Once on the inside, they would gorge themselves on trail mix, granola bars, or whatever was available. On more than one occasion, we returned from fishing to find they had infiltrated some bag or another, despite our attempts to keep it free from critters.

One afternoon, during a rousing match of Hacky Sack, we had a chipmunk wander into our circle. Not being able to resist, we decided to have a little fun at the expense of the poor little rodent. "Keep him in the circle," Paul shouted. As the chipmunk sensed he was surrounded, he began to scamper toward an opening between us. The two players nearest this exit point quickly closed the gap and the chipmunk darted back into the circle. Then, it took another course and sprinted toward a different opening, which was quickly closed again.

In order to liven up the pace a bit, we all began stamping our feet like some sort of deranged powwow as the chipmunk accelerated his escape-attempt frenzy. He pinballed between the four of us, frantically searching for an escape while we carried out our sadistic game of chipmunk Hacky Sack. Back and forth and back again he went, until after about forty seconds, we began to tire of our torment and finally let him scamper back to the woods with his heart racing at redline. While we all knew our teasing was a tad sick, we also felt it was a bit of justice for some of the annoyances these critters had caused us in the past.

Our other forms of downtime entertainment were pretty mundane. We often played cards around the fire. On some of the later nights, we would let the dealer invent his own new games, like ten-card stud with four wild cards. It was always interesting, but we quickly found out how hard it was to keep track of four wild cards. Another one was Double Black Jack, where the goal was to get to forty-two, not twenty-one. We came up with some interesting variations indeed. The rules were never written down and, thus, were lost forever. This was probably a good thing.

Reading, for whatever reason, was never a top priority on these vacations. It's a bit strange that it wasn't, as we were all college-educated men and were all pretty voracious readers. It might have had something to do with our ages at the time. The only book I recall seeing in our years up north was Paul's tattered copy of *Trout Fishing in America,* by Richard Brautigan. I remember picking it up and reading his description of a creek that looked "like 12,845 telephone booths in a row with high Victorian ceilings and all the doors taken off and all the backs of the booths knocked out." To me it was literary genius. That book got me started reading the writings of the whole beat generation.

Paul also always picked up a couple of tabloids like the *Star* and *National Enquirer* during our pretrip shopping ventures. In the store, we shook our heads at his apparent disregard for intellectual stimuli in favor of the literary equivalent of Twinkies. Of course, by the end of the week, we had each read those tabloids at least twice. After four days in the woods, the *Enquirer* reads like Shakespeare and the *Star* like Walt Whitman.

Aliens Visit the White House.

To be, or not to be.

Ultimately, after getting passed around the group a time or two, these tabloids ended up being burned as fire starters, which seemed a fitting end for such drivel.

*   *   *

Unlike the high school trips I took years earlier, these trips were always electronic-free. We didn't bring radios, tape players, or Walkmans—the iPods of the '80s, for those of you too young to remember. Of course, cell phones weren't invented yet, so they were neither an issue nor a distraction. It was universally agreed upon that being unplugged for a week was a good thing. The silence of the Boundary Waters was refreshing to our souls and we knew that all the electronic noise would be waiting for us when the week was over.

There were times, though, that the noise followed me into the wilderness and pursued me relentlessly. It always took the form of a single song that haunted me the whole week long—an earworm that could not be shaken. Usually it was a song that I heard on the car stereo on the way up. With Paul being in a band, me being a music lover, and Rob and Keith being hard of hearing, we tended to listen to music at earsplitting levels for much of the car ride. It served to kind of weld certain songs to your synapses so that no degree of silence could shake them loose. In fact, the silence of the woods often amplified the effect of a nonstop tune. Without the white noise of the city, there was nothing to drown out the song skipping through your skull over and over ad nauseam.

One year in particular, the song was U2's "Another Time, Another Place." This song is a great, driving rock anthem—their best song ever, in my opinion. A multitude of classic guitar solos and transitional bridge moments in the song make it simple to commit to memory. Too simple, in my case. I must have replayed parts of the song in my head a hundred times a day for most of the trip. Sometimes it would be the fade-in guitar intro. Other times it would be the middle part where Bono holds a note for a few seconds. Still other times it would be a searing guitar solo near the end of the song.

It usually started first thing in the morning and went for most of the day. It functioned as a cheap form of entertainment at first. There were times in the day when it broke the monotony of sitting around camp. In the middle of digging through a pack, there would be Bono wailing, "Weeeeee lie, another time, another place. Weeeeee lie . . . "

It's such a great song and I love music, so I actually welcomed the intrusion into the quiet. After a while though, it began to get annoying. It was a bit like the teenage kid who played the same song over and over in his room to the point where his parents wanted to scream, "Turn that thing off!" The problem was, I couldn't turn it off. I tried thinking of other songs, I tried ignoring it, and I tried napping it out of my head, but nothing worked. I'd wake up and there it was, "Weeeeee lie, another time, another place." I began to wish I was in another time and another place. Eventually, I came to terms with the fact that at least it was a good song and not something sappy by Air Supply.

The following year, the earworm was a Grateful Dead song. It manifested itself mostly in the form of long, winding guitar solos by Jerry Garcia. The year after that, it was the song "Valerie Loves Me," by Material Issue. In it, the singer talks about a girl who has no time for him, despite his delusions otherwise. The song starts with a bouncy happy beat and builds to a point where he maniacally screams, "Valerie loves me!!!" That one about drove me insane. It only took a week to ruin a good song forever.

When I told Paul about my struggles with my radio-head obsession year after year, he said he often experienced the same thing. He said there's something about the pairing of words with music that allows the brain to remember every little nuance of a song, every subtle chord change, the timing of the pauses—everything.

The brain is an amazing, mysterious, and wonderful thing. Regrettably, it has no mute button.

The Cleaning

Being in the woods for an extended period of time can cause a person to become immune to his own scent. This is not a good thing. When you're outdoors with other men who aren't overly concerned with their own hygiene, you tend to become a bit lax about all things related to soap. Because we always shared the close proximity of a two-man tent, there was an unwritten rule that each man would take the proper steps to avoid tented asphyxiations.

The bathing process involved a preliminary check of the area to see if any canoeists were traveling in your direction. No sense in scaring or causing temporary blindness to an unsuspecting fellow camper. The next step involved stripping to your underwear, grabbing a bar of soap, and either diving or wading into the lake. (I understand that this is not an ecologically sound practice anymore, but regrettably, what's done is done. In my defense, we did use Ivory, which was the mildest soap of the day.) On some rare occasions, those less modest would go au naturel. Once in, you would lather up and then duck under the water to rinse off. It usually didn't happen for any of us until the second or third day. During that early fall time of year, the lakes were cold, and time spent in them was usually done out of necessity rather than desire.

Finding a suitable area to bathe in was never a sure thing. The drop-offs from shore were often steep and not conducive to wading. Other times the shallows were simply too rocky to negotiate. In these situations we typically delayed the bathing process for another campsite on another day. Most of the time, another day really couldn't make matters much worse anyway.

I recall one trip where, despite the poor shoreline area for bathing, most of us were at a point where we *needed* to do something to clean ourselves up. Washing your face lakeside with a washcloth and soap only got you so far. It made you feel a little better, but to feel fully normal again required complete immersion. A poor man's shower or a farmer's shower, call it what you will, can change your whole outlook on life, for a moment anyway. We were at the point in our trip where we needed that new outlook.

The lake bottom at this site was strewn with sharp, algae-covered rocks. Some of them were flat, which helped, but negotiating them still required balance and skill. Paul and I slowly waded out into the water in our boxer shorts, hoping to wash away two days' buildup of sweat, sun block, and bug spray. I ventured out first, stepping slowly and cautiously. Occasionally, I'd hit a slippery or sharp rock and end up windmilling my arms wildly in an attempt to keep my balance. The rocks were slick, for sure, but there was a strange allure to the challenge of navigating the dolomite minefield in front of us in the name of better hygiene.

Somewhere about thigh level, I stopped so I could soap up. Paul followed in the shallower water behind me. For reasons unknown, we didn't all have our own individual bars of soap on this particular trip. Perhaps with the lack of attention to hygiene and the ever-conscious attempt to pack light, we may have decided that one or two bars was enough for the group. Whatever the case, because of my perilous stance on the slippery rocks I said, "Hey, hand me the soap, would ya?" and reached around blindly to Paul so he could hand it to me.

"Here you go, Jimbo," he said.

I brought my hand around to see not a bar of soap but rather a grey, gnarly crayfish! Crayfish are the freshwater crustaceans of the lakes up north. They're small greyish critters complete with ratcheted armor-like tails, long antennae, and pincers capable of giving you a good squeeze, if provoked. They are the distant, ugly, dwarf cousin of the lobster. The whole species is an evolutionary oversight as far as I'm concerned.

When I saw the creature in my hand, I did my best to maintain my outdoor masculine composure by screaming, "Aaaaiiiiiieeeee!"

With my palm locked open, I flung the poor creature out into the deep water in an embarrassing display of cowardice. I have always had a fear of crayfish, crabs, and lobsters, or any creature with antennae, for that matter. They are aquatic spiders to me, best left under the rocks they call home.

It was after I hurled the crustacean when things got entertaining. I flung the crayfish with such force that I was thrown completely off balance. First my right foot slid off its slimy foothold, and then the left followed. As I stumbled, trying to regain my balance, it seemed that every rock I stepped on was either sharper or slicker than the one before. My arms took on jerking dance-like movements as I attempted to bring myself under control. It was probably a lot like watching Joe Cocker at Woodstock or maybe the Frankenstein monster after he was exposed to fire. The difference in both cases was that my words were intelligible. As I recall, most of them were brief, colorful, and four letters in length, shooting out of my mouth with semi-automatic regularity.

I'd like to say that this is the point in the story where Paul rushed to my aid to help keep me from falling, but alas, it wasn't to be. It seems he was too busy watching my flagman impersonation to be of any useful assistance. He, along with Rob and Keith on shore, was in hysterics and seemed to be fresh out of empathy. So for ten seconds I was left to my own devices, flailing, stepping, cursing, flailing, stepping, cursing.

I eventually found my footing and regained my balance. Paul apologized, saying, "Oops. Sorry, Jimbo. I thought that was the soap."

His apology would have been fully accepted if it hadn't come delivered with an ear-to-ear grin.

"No, really, Jim, I'm sorry about that," he said, laughing mightily. He was having serious trouble containing himself.

"Jim, you should have kept it. We could have used it for bait," Rob chimed in, not wanting to be left out of the beatdown. As was often the case in our family, I was the source of entertainment and amusement for the rest of the crowd. It was a role I knew well and had become accustomed to. In this day and age, people often say, "You were lucky to grow up in a big family."

Lucky indeed.

The Leaving

Many of our trips out of the Boundary Waters took us several portages deep and, a few days later, we were paddling and portaging our way back using the same route. This required revisiting the difficult portages that we cursed only days earlier. Having been through the portages once, we knew what lay ahead and took them on with a sense of determination. Thoughts of sleeping in real beds also played a role in our newfound focus.

Of all the trips we took over the years, only two stand out as having memorable conclusions. The first involved a trip across Snowbank Lake to reach the launch where our vehicles were parked. Snowbank is big, covering over four thousand acres with a depth of over a hundred and fifty feet in some places. Because of its sheer size and depth, it can get extremely rough in even a slight wind.

We had just portaged out from a rough. windy trip on Boot Lake to find that the conditions were even more perilous on Snowbank. Small whitecaps formed in the middle and dared us to take on the challenge. Being on the last lake on the last day of our trip made us pocket our sensibilities in favor of reaching our destination on schedule. The thought of spending an unplanned night in a tent as opposed to our own beds back home was not an attractive option.

"Well, this looks like it could be interesting." I said with a hint of trepidation in my voice.

"Put your life jackets on," Paul said. He didn't need to remind us. We all had a healthy respect for the water and were certainly on board with the idea of life jackets. If there was any hint of danger, we were all quick to take the proper precautions so as to avoid disaster.

We briefly discussed our projected travel route based on the wind direction, and after we secured the gear and buckled our life vests, we set out on the frothy waters. We paddled hard southwesterly into a strong north wind that worked to push us off our course. Anyone who has paddled a canoe in a heavy wind knows the frustration of trying to keep the front end from catching the wind and succumbing to it. It's hard work for both people in the canoe. Working together is essential. The person in the bow not only has to struggle with paddling twice as hard but is also forced to paddle almost exclusively on the side to which the wind is blowing them. This offsets the pushing effect of the wind, but it also results in fatigue in the arm that is working the paddle shaft on that side.

The guy in the stern has his own issues in strong winds and big water. He is charged with keeping the insubordinate canoe not only upright but also pointed in the correct line of travel. He must paddle much harder than normal and make the relevant rudder adjustments only as needed so as to not lose precious momentum. If the canoe takes on a zigzag course, he looks bad and his bowman gets testy.

After about fifteen minutes of hard paddling, we were in the middle of the lake. Suddenly, the water took on a new energy. The waves rolled big and deep, lifting the canoe and tossing it like a chew toy. I began thinking maybe another night in a tent wouldn't be such a bad idea after all. On occasion, the canoe's front end landed on the water with a *thwack*! This served as an auditory reminder that if we didn't already have our spiritual lives in order, now would be a good time to start.

Keith and I were the bowmen for our canoes, and at this point were both suffering from what I call whitecap hypnosis. This is an affliction caused by large, daunting waves that play mind games with canoeists, shocking them into a trancelike state. Paralyzed by both fear and wonder at the sheer magnitude of the waves, the canoeists freeze in midstroke at the sight of some of the high rollers. This not only serves to irk the partner in the stern, but it also allows the wind to change the canoe's course and thus win the battle between man and lake. You have to stay on top of the waves, or they will get on top of you.

I became aware of this state and made a conscious effort to fight through it and continue to paddle. We all encouraged Keith to focus and paddle too. Keith was *not* a swimmer, and while he did not fear the water, he preferred to keep a layer of aluminum between himself and it. To his credit, he worked hard through the waves when it was needed most. We pushed onward for about thirty minutes in the wind and the waves. Our saving grace was a large island that lay about three quarters of the way across, not far from the canoe launch. We tucked behind the leeward side of this island, where the water was much calmer. We all set down our paddles and took a much-needed break from the wind and paddling. Keith turned around toward our canoe and said, "Man, that wind sucked!"

"No lie. What'd you think of those waves?" I asked.

"They sucked too!" Keith replied.

The island provided a nice wind block and was an incredible respite for all of us. We were physically exhausted and grateful to not have to struggle just to maintain our position. We relaxed, passed around the canteens of Surfin' Berry Kool-Aid, and just rested for a while. When we recovered from our battle we continued on, knowing full well that we were facing a four-hour drive ahead of us. At this point, the launch was only a ten-minute paddle away and we were able to finish the trip unscathed. No overturned canoes or loss of life, thanks in part to good old-fashioned muscle and teamwork. It was this kind of risky adventure that singed images of our Boundary Waters experience into my brain, images that I still draw upon and relish to this day.

The other notable ending came in 1990 when all four brothers managed to make it for the trip as well as our friends Brad and Keith.

We had just landed the canoes at our destination at the Snowbank Lake launch and happened to encounter some other canoeists. Sensing the photographic opportunity, Rob went to the truck and got his camera. He asked the campers if they would take a picture of us, and they happily obliged.

The four of us brothers and Brad and Keith formed up by the canoes and gave our best "home from the woods" smiles. We were unshaven, unwashed, and for the most part, shirtless, probably much like the trappers and traders of generations long ago. Some had hands on hips, others had thumbs hooked in their pockets, and we wore a mix of jeans, shorts, and a couple of dirty shirts. It was no glamour shot for sure, but it was iconic in that it was the first showing all four of us together in an outdoor setting for as long as any of us could remember.

Much like photos of my father and his brothers, it's one of those pictures that will likely surface for generations, long after we're gone. A look at the picture reveals that there is no mistaking that we're related. All of us standing tall, confident, lean, and muscular illustrates that, while similar, each of us had his own unique swatch of our father's cloth hopelessly woven into his fabric. The shot was a reminder that, while we had our differences, we knew the importance of remaining in touch with what was common among us—our father and his outdoor heritage.

*   *   *

The drives home were always long, nap-filled affairs. Unlike the music-filled, festive trips up, the drives home were far more restrained and had fewer stops. We had a tendency to set the cruise control a couple miles per hour faster as well. Talk was sporadic and came in short bursts, as we spent much of our time thinking about all that we were going back to. The reality of our realities was coming into focus with every passing mile.

Because we had to return the canoes and equipment to Courage North, we typically stopped there for a night, unpacked, and got a decent night's sleep. After much-needed hot showers, we each took a separate room in the main lodge of the camp. Even though we had no sheets or bedding in the rooms, which were already winterized, it was always a welcome change to have a mattress and a real pillow to lay your head on. A day earlier in the woods, all we had was a quarter-inch foam pad between us and the ground and our clothes rolled up in a ball for our pillows. Courage North's rudimentary bunk beds served as a sort of decompression chamber for us, easing us back into the creature comforts at a slower rate.

The next day, we woke and cooked a hearty breakfast of bacon, eggs, pancakes, coffee, and juice. The food was fresh and ash-free, a nice change from the week of eating around the fire pit. Any calories we burned during the week were quickly replenished during these breakfast feasts. We washed it all down with lots of strong coffee. Compared to the sludge we drank around the fire, this tasted like Starbucks and didn't require us straining it through our teeth to filter out the grounds.

After breakfast we finished cleaning and packing away the equipment we borrowed from Courage North. Everyone pitched in on the cleaning, in part because we had been calling each other out all week when one or the other was caught slacking. By the end of the week, we were all pretty much in tune with what needed to be done. The sooner we finished, the sooner we would be headed home. Once the packing was done and the main sleeping areas were put back to normal, we thanked our gracious hosts, who oversaw the camp, and got on the road. It was always a long, forgettable four-hour drive down the interstate, ending with our jubilant arrival at home.

Once we were back in the Twin Cities, the drivers would drop each of us off at our various residences. Because we were all technically still on vacation, we usually arranged to meet at a local watering hole later that evening to relive the events of the week, shoot some pool, and haggle over any debts owed. I remember these nights as upbeat gatherings. We put aside petty grievances we may have built up with each other over the week and just celebrated the closing of another successful trip as brothers and friends.

Returning from the remote wilderness of the Boundary Waters was always a difficult thing for me, for a couple of reasons. When I was in the deep wilderness with not much more than the food, clothing, and shelter I needed, all carried on my back, it took freedom to a new level. The woods had a way of making me realize that the material excesses and creature comforts we all take for granted only make us soft and flabby. In the backcountry you were lean and mean. I'd get over the melancholy feelings soon enough, but I always started the countdown to next year's trip as soon as I was back home.

Another cause for the post-trip depression was that, unlike my brothers, who all lived in close proximity to each other in St. Paul, I had to return *alone* to Milwaukee. The long hours we spent camping together meant conversations broke the surface a bit more than at the holidays and other times I returned to visit. We talked about crazy times growing up as kids together, sharing bedrooms and hand-me-downs in our old house on Portland Avenue. We talked about college and careers, dreams and girlfriends. It was a chance to get to know them as adults and reconnect with them on a deeper level than "pass the turkey" and "how about those Vikings?"

This is not to say the experiences were all joyous, feel-good times. There were trips when five days together was a couple too many. But there was something undeniably cool about hanging with adult family in the wild. It might have been because I could picture my dad doing the same thing with his brothers. In that respect, maybe it was an attempt to connect with someone long since gone or to try to fill some hole in my heart.

In any case, I look back on those early years in the Boundary Waters with my brothers with great fondness and gratitude. We were all at the point in our lives where we were each starting to make a name for ourselves in our jobs and were all on the crest of serious relationships with our future brides. We were still footloose and fiancée free, as my friend Pat used to refer to it, and the Boundary Waters was the perfect place to burn off excess youthful energy and reconnect.

At the same time, without even knowing it, we were forging an unbreakable bond between us that would stand the test of time. While we didn't always see eye to eye in every situation, we respected each other enough to agree to disagree. We worked together through many challenges, each of them serving as another rivet in the steel fabric of the brotherhood. The laughs we shared echo through time the same way they did across the many lakes we traveled together. The memories we created are ours alone and now reside in the shadows of our father, who loved this area as much as we did.

I only wish he could have been there, too.

Part III: Children

Our Return – 2009

For a number of reasons, there was an eighteen-year break since my last venture to the Boundary Waters Canoe Area. As much as we enjoyed the trips and the family bonding that went with them, marriages, houses, job changes, and kids became new priorities for all of us and the annual tradition fell by the wayside. The years rolled by and before we knew it, almost two decades had passed since we had been there together.

That's not to say we hadn't made individual trips up to the area. Rob, younger than me by two years, had been up a time or two with some of his friends. Tom seemed to go nearly every year, often taking his son and daughter up with him. Personally, though, I had not been up since the last trip in 1991.

I've always envied that all of them were close enough to the BWCA that they could make a long weekend of it and still make it work. I had at least a ten-hour drive to get to the area, more than double what it took them. Couple the long drive with all the new life changes and commitments and I just never found the chance to get back. I told Tom and Rob that I would love the chance to join them with one or both of my kids, if they ever saw the opportunity. My hopes were realized during the winter of 2008, when Tom, Rob, and I started planning our first father/son/daughter Boundary Waters trip.

Tom has two children, Hunter and Jocelyn. Because of his love of all things field and stream, his kids have been exposed to the great outdoors since they were babies. Hunter grew up with a fishing rod in his hand and even has a photo journal of many of the fish he's caught. His universe revolves around his next outing, whether it is hunting, hiking, or sitting in a portable fishing shack on a frozen lake.

Despite Tom's attempts to convince her, Jocelyn doesn't share their zeal for the rigors of camping and fishing.

Alison and Amanda are Rob's kids. Alison, who is close in age to my daughter Sarah, grew up fishing at the cabin with her dad and cousins and has the patience necessary to be successful at it. Amanda, like Jocelyn, is not as keen on the whole outdoor experience but tends to find ways to amuse herself if she gets bored with the outdoor activity at hand.

Because of their trips to the cabin and campouts with the cousins, my kids, Sarah and Ben, both appreciate the outdoors as well. I'll never forget seeing Sarah as a five-year-old, crouched on the dock at the cabin, wearing her life vest, holding her Snoopy pole, and catching bluegills as fast as I could bait her hook. Ben doesn't have the same level of patience for fishing, but his love for all things camping is very apparent. Give him a pocket knife and a stick and he'll whittle a spear while dreaming of taking down a deer from fifty yards.

"Keep it simple" was our philosophy for this first foray into the rugged wilderness. One of our concerns was putting the kids through too much, thereby spoiling their desire to ever return. It was decided the youngest girls, Amanda and Jocelyn, would stay behind with our wives at a friend's condo in Two Harbors. For some reason, shopping, sightseeing, and a condo on the shores of Lake Superior had more appeal than sleeping on the ground in the middle of nowhere. Imagine that.

In keeping with the simplicity theme, we decided it would be a short, two-night, three-day trip. Additionally, we would traverse only one short portage. On the trips of years before, we would often tackle several of these in a day. Tough portages can challenge a person's love of the outdoors, so we opted to not go there. Since we would be doing the bulk of the heavy lifting, Tom, Rob, and I, all in our late forties and early fifties, saw the benefits all the way around. None of us needed to be reminded we weren't twenty-seven anymore. We agreed that, while it's good to prove your masculinity by carrying a canoe on your shoulders for long distances, there's no sense in belaboring the point. This was a vacation, after all.

Because he's done Boundary Waters trips for so many years, Tom is the quintessential BW camper. He packs small, travels light, and is well prepared for most anything. For this particular trip, he shared one of the secrets to his success: an equipment spreadsheet. During a series of e-mail exchanges prior to our trip, Tom attached this list to help Rob and I plan what to bring. Organized by category—food, clothing, canoe gear, cooking items, etc.—it was comprehensive and proved to be a great help.

On his printed copy of the list, Tom had even taken things to the next level by handwriting a single letter next to each item that referenced *where* the item was packed. P stood for his main pack, F for his food pack, and so on. While this might seem overkill for some, if you've ever camped, you know a good portion of your time is spent looking for stuff. This list alleviated much of that. The exception, of course, is when you forget where you put the list, in which case the whole system goes up in flames. Sometimes you need a list for the list.

Tom chose the route we would take and secured the BWCA camping permits. Sawbill Lake at the end of the Sawbill Trail was to be our entry point. None of us had ever been up this particular trail, so it seemed like a good way to get a feel for the area. The other benefit was that Sawbill Outfitters was located at the launch. This provided us a place to rent some equipment and talk to the staff about important things like what the fish were biting on and where. Alton Lake, a short hundred-and-fifty-yard portage away from the launch, was to be our ultimate destination. Alton had a dozen or so campsites and, according to Tom's research, held the promise of better fishing than Sawbill. Tom was usually right about such matters, so we trusted his judgment and started our planning. This route would also give the kids a gentle taste of the portaging process and would serve to ease them into the total BW experience.

Two Plans Are Better Than One

Much of the pretrip planning was done using e-mail. Additional details were discussed in a ten-minute conversation during a family party at our sister's house the night before we packed. I doubt Lewis and Clark got where they did by strategizing with a beer cup in their hand, but somehow it all worked out for us. It was less than ideal preparation, as I'll explain later, but completely in line with the shotgun-type preparation of eighteen years earlier.

Tom's instructions for meals relegated me to cover one breakfast, Rob one dinner, and Tom one breakfast and one dinner. All of us would be responsible for sandwich lunches for ourselves and our kids. He also made recommendations for the meals—brats and hot dogs for dinner and bacon and eggs for breakfast.

Taking to heart his recommendations, Rob and I headed to SuperTarget to do the shopping on Sunday afternoon. It seemed so much more sterile, scripted, and responsible than our late-night, barley-and-hop-fueled shopping trips of so long ago. Shopping after midnight on the night before a trip with three other guys and with a few beers under your belt is not just a job, it's an adventure. Shopping at SuperTarget at two in the afternoon on the day before your trip just seemed so vanilla in comparison. Then again, waking up the next morning was considerably easier, so there was that.

Rob picked up the dinner items as suggested, while I focused on the breakfast food. Knowing my kids' eating habits, I picked up two packages of Pop-Tarts, figuring they would, at a minimum, make a nice snack. Nothing says great north woods like processed white flour and artificial fruit filling. Needless to say, they were a hit at almost any time of the day. Ben even went so far as to ask if he could heat his up in a skillet over the fire, an idea I quickly dismissed. This wasn't the Holiday Inn. We were roughing it. Eat it cold, like the voyageurs would. It builds character.

This is not to say I condone or recommend processed, sugar-laden food as a substitute for healthy, nutritious fare in the woods. However, I've found that sometimes the best philosophy when kids are involved is "whatever works." I would have loved for them to forage for their own edible mushrooms and sphagnum moss for a delicious, hearty outback stew, but I was a realist, too. Pop-Tarts all around it was. Whatever works.

Despite our search, we were unable to find any Surfin' Berry Punch Kool-Aid, our powdered drink choice of yesteryear. Instead, we settled for individual packets of Crystal Light the kids could pour into their personal water bottles. This turned out to be a much more sanitary way to drink than when, years before, we settled for a simple wipe of the canteen spout with our sleeve before passing it on to the next guy. Mmmmm . . . yummy.

We shopped for the usual items of past trips: hot chocolate, granola bars, coffee, trail mix, and beef jerky. The jerky was the bagged, mass-produced kind that was more like beef bacon strips than the thick, delicious top sirloin we'd indulged in during our younger days. Assuredly, it was the only kind of jerky our kids knew, so we decided to stick with what worked. We topped the shopping trip off with an eight-pack of Miller beer in plastic bottles. The Miller was proof positive we were roughing it. While it was fine twenty years ago, my tastes have matured and these days I only buy it if nothing else is available. Because cans and glass are not allowed inside the Boundary Waters, we were left with the bottom of the barrel, so to speak—Miller beer in plastic bottles. No quality microbrews here. Remember, this was not the Holiday Inn.

During the packing session that night, Tom paid a quick visit to finalize a few details and drop off one of the canoes for Rob to haul up with his truck.

"What'd you get for dinner, Rob?" Tom inquired.

"Brats, hot dogs, and beans," Rob replied.

"That's the same thing I got!" Tom said, laughing.

This is a textbook example of how the whole planning process falls down in our family. When Tom recommended brats, hot dogs, and beans, we never took it to mean he was recommending them to *himself*. Of course, a phone call ahead of time would have prevented this duplication but, after all, we are brothers, and we deal much better with one another on a level of broad assumptions and wild-assed guesses. So we ended up with the same meal for the two nights of our trip.

Whatever works.

In the e-mail planning exchange, it was also decided Rob would drive his truck and haul one canoe, and Tom would drive his Toyota 4Runner and haul the other two canoes. Unlike the sometimes-decrepit vehicles of the past, these were both fairly reliable trucks. Being true to form for our adventure, however, one of them was not without flaw.

When we showed up at Tom's house, we were a bit surprised to see he had crafted luggage-rack extensions out of two-by-fours to allow for two canoes to ride atop his truck. It was strikingly similar to the custom-made hillbilly rack we'd built for Rob's Malibu twenty years prior. Tom was not part of that trip, yet he used almost identical materials to accomplish the same result. Evidently great minds think alike. In any case, while this rack turned out to serve the purpose quite well, it also lent a degree of uncertainty, risk, and danger to the trip that took me back to the days of the old Malibu. Watching the extensions bow when Tom hit a bump and then visualizing the probable chain of events that would transpire if one of them snapped made for some interesting tailgating.

By my guess, I imagined the first two-by-four would snap at seventy miles per hour, meaning the canoe would fall to that side, thereby taking on wind and creating a sort of canoe drag chute. After a second or two, the front rope would fray and snap and the canoe would likely shift and become perpendicular to the truck and impale the windshield of the vehicle next to it. At this point, the two vehicles would become conjoined and form a high-speed, double-wide, no-passing zone. And that is the better of the two scenarios. If no one was in the left lane, the canoe would likely fly entirely off and come windmilling end over end down the highway toward our vehicle.

I'll admit that any napping I did was with one eye open.

Along with the custom-rack integrity question, Rob and I noticed that the left rear tire was low. I began to fret about it a bit, fearing it would blow and put our vacation on hold while it was fixed. I was having a Malibu flashback. Later that morning, we stopped at a café in Two Harbors for breakfast and, as I was eating, I mentioned the low tire to Tom.

He said with disturbing nonchalant, "Oh yeah, it's had a slow leak for a while now."

In our family, some things never change.

Adventure 101

The trips of years before usually had their share of equipment calamities and near disasters. This trip proved no different. The first incident occurred early in the trip by the doing of my own hand. While packing all of our equipment, I carefully put both of my kids' low-budget digital cameras into a fabric case toward the top of my main pack. We loaded our equipment into the canoes and got ready to push out from the dock. Sarah and I were in one canoe, Rob and Alison were in another, and Tom took Hunter and Ben in his. Before we left the launch, I decided to get some photos of the start of our adventure. I pulled out one of the cameras, snapped a few pictures, and quickly laid the case on top of the flap on the large pack in front of me.

After a short twenty-minute paddle, we approached our portage. Tom and Rob landed their canoes in front of us a couple of minutes earlier and were unloading on shore. As we approached the landing, I told Sarah to paddle hard so we could beach the canoe with a head of steam. We dug our paddles in hard and suddenly hit a large submerged rock with a *thunk*! A shock rippled through the canoe and we came to an abrupt stop. The camera case rolled off the pack and into the lake. I could hardly believe my eyes as it bobbed tauntingly on the surface, slowly taking on water. I back-paddled aggressively, trying to position us closer to the case.

"Sarah, back-paddle, the cameras are in the water!" I shouted to my daughter.

"What? Oh no, Dad, is that my camera or Ben's?" she asked in a panic.

"Actually, it's both of them," I said.

She started back-paddling frantically. After what seemed an eternity, though it really was no more than fifteen seconds, I was able to grab the case strap and hoist it aboard. The case was saturated and a cursory look showed things did not look promising for the cameras. Once we landed, I assessed the damage, and the prognosis was dire. Water was behind the LCD screen on both cameras and there were no signs of life from either. Sarah and Ben were disappointed but hung their hopes on the thought that I would replace the cameras eventually. I spent the rest of the trip drying the cameras out using various techniques. I tried everything from wrapping them in towels to literally hanging them on the clothesline in the sun. It was a complete rerun of the canoe-tipping, camera-dunking incident of almost twenty years prior.

It was then that the self-loathing set in. Hadn't I learned anything about packing valuables safely away during transport from past trips? On the trip of '88, when my nice single-lens reflex camera got dunked, I vowed to always take precautions with valuables in the future. *Why, no Ziploc bags for them?* I thought. I was pretty hard on myself, as I should have been. One of the fundamental givens of canoeing is to assume that everything that can get wet will get wet. I knew that and should have planned for it. In any case, I tried to use my bad planning as a teachable moment for my kids and moved on. Thankfully, Tom and Rob shared their pictures with me after the trip was over.

Déjà View

This trip I was careful to make sure I kept better track of my glasses. I did not want to repeat the experience of losing and then finding them again during that fateful portage in the late '80s. I kept them on during our portage and through most of our day, in part because my vision declined to the point of needing them for everything but reading. In keeping with the tradition of trashing equipment and personal effects, however, I did have a momentary lapse of reason that proved to be costly in the long run.

On the morning we were to leave, Tom was cooking breakfast while I sat with my back against a fallen log that was used as a bench around the fire pit. As a practice, we draped our life vests on the log as makeshift backrests when we sat on the ground. Sitting for long periods hunched over with no back support in a canoe or around the fire made these simple chairs a welcome change. I picked up a magazine I brought along and started paging through it. I took off my glasses and carefully placed them on the life vest to my left, thinking they would be safe until I needed them again. Shortly into my reading, I was distracted by some menial task that needed attention. When I returned to my seat a few minutes later, I couldn't find my glasses. Unsure as to where I had set them down, I began to look around camp. I checked my shave kit, my pack, and my tent. No joy. Being fairly sure I'd taken them off by my chair, I looked around it a second time and found they were underneath the life vest that I set them on. The vest was no longer neatly laid on the log but appeared to have been sat on at some point.

My wire-rimmed glasses looked like they had taken a few spins in a garbage disposal. The left arm was bent at an angle thirty degrees from its origin. The right arm had about a ten-degree bend in the opposite direction. The nose pads were bent inward, not completely flat, but close.

"Ah, eeee, oooohhh, wha? How? But I . . . they were just . . . ahhhhheee . . . son of a . . . What the?"

I searched for words, but all I could do was sputter unintelligible nonsense.

I took a deep breath and tried to rationalize that it wasn't really that bad and that they could probably be bent back into wearable shape. I started with the nose pads, which were easily pried back to their original position. Next, I took to bending the arms, which were bent where they met the hinge. I bent and prayed and bent some more. I tried them on and felt like one of my eyes was out of place and needed to be more like in the middle of my cheek. Like Ralphie in *A Christmas Story* after he broke his glasses with his BB gun, I thought, "I'll fake it. No one will ever notice."

"Dad, what's wrong with your glasses?" Sarah asked when I saw her a minute later.

So much for going under the radar.

"Someone sat on them, I think."

"They're crooked," she said, intending to enlighten me to the obvious.

"Yeah, I know. Thanks for noticing. That's what happens when they get sat on," I said with crimson sarcasm.

After further investigation, I learned Ben was the last person to sit on that particular life vest. It wasn't his fault and I knew it. It was no one's fault but mine. Luckily, they were still wearable. I looked a bit off-kilter for the rest of the trip, but I realized if I tilted my head a bit to the left at all times, I actually looked balanced. Puzzled, yes, but balanced. The entire escapade was a reminder you should never bring anything camping you don't mind losing, burning, drenching, bending, shorting, or disassembling.

Just don't do it.

Weathering the Storm

On this trip, we were blessed with almost-perfect weather. The only precipitation came on the first day, when we were fishing. The cover overhead did not look like rain clouds, but that was likely tainted by the goggles of optimism one tends to wear on the first day of any outdoor vacation. It started easily enough as a few refreshing sprinkles. Over time, the rain coming from the non–rain clouds came down a bit harder. It quickly evolved from a refreshing sprinkle into an annoying drizzle. Attempts to justify our apparent indifference to the weather quickly began cropping up. Sayings like, "The fish bite better when it's raining," or "Fish love these weather fronts," were beginning to take on water of their own.

Eventually the rain became more consistent, so we relented and headed back to camp. When we landed, it was like a scene from the beaches of Normandy. Kids and adults all scrambled out of the boats, leaving a debris field of rods, bait, and life vests in their path. I quickly located the rain ponchos and a large plastic tarp inside the equipment pack underneath a towering white pine. After the adults made sure the camp gear was covered, all seven of us huddled under our makeshift shelter for ten minutes until the skies cleared.

It was a scene right out of a trip from so many years ago—a trip where the brothers all had to seek shelter during a dinnertime cloudburst that drove us underneath a tarp. We huddled there, everyone holding a corner of the tarp and digging into a pot of beans that had been warming on the fire. The only thing different in the 2009 version were a few of the characters and the missing beans. It was at this point that a couple things occurred to me.

One was how, as a family, you all pull together when things get tough. Here we were, seven blood relatives, all Landwehrs, huddled under our Hurricane Katrina model home with nothing but each other to rely on. When the going gets tough, everyone grabs a corner of the tarp and holds on. It seemed almost metaphorical for the way our family weathered things like the early deaths of our father and sister.

The other revelation wrought from the tarp gathering was how my brothers had become such great fathers. All four of us love our kids and want to instill in them the love of outdoors and their families. This is not to say we're perfect, but given the absence of a father for much of our childhoods and the fact we're all winging this fatherhood thing, I'd have to say at this point, we're doing pretty well.

Walleye Chopped

Another memorable weather-related incident took place on the second day of the trip when we went out fishing after dinner. It was a windy evening, creating a condition known as the "walleye chop." This is when the breeze causes enough wave action to push walleye to feed more aggressively than they do in calm water, or at least that is the lore behind the phrase. We were looking forward to seeing if the weather might help our luck a bit.

Having spent the earlier part of the day paddling the two girls around, Rob decided this evening he would pair up with Ben, thinking it would mean less work on his part. I offered to take the girls in my canoe to give Rob a break. What he later realized was, given the conditions, having a third person in your canoe was actually beneficial. The added weight enabled you to hold a truer course and prevented your bow from catching the wind.

As we battled against the wind, Sarah spoke up, saying, "This stupid wind keeps blowing us the wrong way, Dad."

"I know, hon, but keep it up, or we'll end up getting turned again."

"I am, but I'm just sayin'," she replied.

"If you think we've got it hard, look at Uncle Rob and Ben. They're getting beat up by this wind."

Sarah and Alison both looked over at my brother and son and chuckled a little. Rob, stuck with the lightest kid in the group, was battling the wind with great fervor. A couple of times, he encouraged Ben to try to improve their position or correct their course. Ben, to his credit, did his best to help, but his youth and inexperience neutralized his efforts. They looked like a floating weather vane, struggling against but ultimately succumbing to the whims of the wind.

After a few minutes of trying to maintain our position to do some fishing, we all agreed we should cross the lake and seek shelter in a protected bay. It was too early to go back to camp and we all wanted to get in some serious fishing. This meant heading directly into the wind and, as a result, meant more metronomic course adjustments by everyone. Eventually we made it across to the bay, which we all agreed was a much better location.

"That wind was fun, wasn't it?" I said to Rob.

"Tell me about it. With Ben in front, I was blowing all over," Rob replied.

"I thought you wanted it that way, with just Ben," I said grinning.

"Very funny, Jim. Very funny," said Rob as he set down his paddle and grabbed his fishing rod.

The years do not take away the fun of chiding a brother.

Loonacy

That same night, once we were in the calmer waters, we turned our focus back to fishing. I grabbed each fishing rod and baited our jigs with leeches. Jigs are brightly colored, painted lead balls with a hook designed to be used with a worm, leech, or minnow. Because leeches are known only to kids as bloodsuckers, it made them very uneasy, and expecting them to put the leeches on the hook was asking too much. Ultimately, it was less work for me to bait them myself than to listen to all the squeamish excuses why they couldn't, so that's what I did.

With hooks baited, we started jigging over the sides of our canoes. The jigging technique involves lightly bouncing your jig off of the bottom of the lake repetitively to lure the fish to your active leech. With walleye fishing, when you feel a gentle tug, you are supposed to count to three and then set the hook with authority. Then, the fun of reeling in the fish begins.

While we jigged away, a loon paddled into our area. They are glorious birds, with their black-and-white checkerboard pattern, striped necks, and black velveteen heads. The swans of the north, they are beautiful and graceful in their natural environment. This one was not shy, and it seemed as interested in us as we were in it.

Fishing was a bit on the slow side, so we all took the opportunity to turn our attention to the approaching loon. Over time, the bird paddled nearer until it was close enough that we could see its deep, ruby-red eyes. It headed toward Tom and Hunter's canoe first and then, from about ten yards away, dove and swam under it. Sensing its motive was to get the walleye on the stringer hanging over the side of the canoe, Tom was Johnny-on-the-spot and yanked the stringer out of the water before the loon could get it. It surfaced, looking agitated that its meal had been snatched away. It leapt out of the water after the dangling walleye, much to Tom's surprise. Again, he yanked it away, laughing at the loon's tenacity.

"Stubborn little bugger, eh?" I yelled.

"I guess," Tom said.

It was a determined creature, however, so it swam away and then circled around, real nonchalant-like, for another try. Tom was on to its intentions, so he kept a diligent watch on the whereabouts of the crazed bird. When it came after the fish a second time, my nephew Hunter armed himself with a canoe paddle, evidently fearing a flyby looning. We quickly informed him that the birds are protected at the state level, regardless of their erratic behavior. Hunter wisely traded the paddle for a camera and ended up with a decent video of "Loon Gone Wild."

Sensing its luck had run out at Tom's boat, the bird decided to try elsewhere and headed toward Rob's. Because he also had a walleye on a stringer, his canoe was a natural attractant. To a loon, it was like dinner on a chain. When the loon dove in the direction of his canoe, Rob said, "Oh no, you don't!" He quickly grabbed the strung fish out of the water and pulled it into the boat. The bird surfaced, surprised and disturbed that it had been foiled again.

"Whoa, you don't really realize how big those things are until you see them up close!" Rob exclaimed.

"Yeah, and they're fast too," I added.

It took a couple more passes at his boat and then decided to see if *my* canoe was the weak link in its food chain. Knowing the routine, I hoisted the two walleye into the bottom of the boat shortly after it dove in our direction. It was fascinating to watch the bird swim deftly under us, seemingly more at home under water than in the air. Its powerful legs, large webbed feet, and hydrodynamic body made it a fast, capable swimmer and a marvel to watch.

Evidently, the third time was our charm, because the loon soon lost interest and pursued other prey. We saw it surface on a couple of occasions with crayfish in its beak, so we were confident it would not return home hungry because of our selfishness.

Anchored Away

Canoes, by design, don't come with anchors, so as a practice we improvised by tying a large rock to a good length of rope for each canoe. No one wants to portage ten pounds of extra weight, so these makeshift solutions gave us a bit of locational stability, which made the fishing much easier. Using them meant we were not constantly adjusting our position because of wind and drift. We were soon to find out these poor-man anchors were not without their drawbacks.

On the same night as the loon adventure, the girls and I were anchored and jigging for walleye. Shortly after we started, Alison managed to get her line snagged on the bottom. Now, when this happens, it is necessary to hoist the anchor so you could pull the boat directly over the snag. This helps the odds of getting your snag loose without losing your jig and, more importantly, your precious leech.

Being in the back of the canoe and being, by default, the anchor man, I reeled in my line and attempted to hoist the anchor. The rock was hopelessly lodged on the bottom, despite my attempts to manhandle it loose.

"What's wrong, Dad?" Sarah inquired.

"The stupid anchor's stuck!"

"Oh, great, and Alison's got a snag," she reminded me.

"Yeah, I know, that's why I'm trying to pull up the anchor, hon," I said with curt authority.

Within seconds, my daughter said, "Oh no, now I have a snag too!"

"Wonderful," I muttered. "I guess the good news is the wind isn't blowing *us* anywhere." The girls laughed at my attempt to make lemonade from the tethered boatload of lemons we'd been dealt.

Rob, a short distance away, asked what I was doing. "Trying to get my rock unstuck," I said. He laughed at my quandary. Again, I felt the love.

After ten minutes of "rock wrasslin'," I managed to free my anchor from the murky depths. Shortly thereafter, I was able to recover Alison's jig and leech by using a series of whipping motions and some G-rated curse words like "Gosh darn," "Gee whiz," and "Holy crap." Sarah's line didn't fare as well. It met an untimely death when I cut it, having expended enough energy dealing with an unforgiving lake bottom. I counted the two out of three recoveries as a victory and moved on to our next location.

As I was positioning our boat into its new spot, I noticed Rob was doing anchor aerobics which looked strikingly similar to the ones I just finished. "Yeah, it sucks, doesn't it?" I laughed and teased, realizing that justice had prevailed. Rob grumbled and continued his upper-body workout. Eventually he freed his rock and resumed fishing. Within five minutes, my rock was stuck again. As I worked with the rope, Rob saw me again and laughed. It seemed there was a developing pattern. The lesson to be learned from the whole episode is that it's okay to revel in another person's misery if you understand they will do the same when your moment comes, because it will.

Oh, yes, it will.

Forest Facilities

Men and boys have it easy in the Boundary Waters when it comes to personal necessity. In a forest full of trees, the facilities for urination are plentiful, clean, and close. The other end of toileting is the great equalizer in the north woods. Latrines in the Boundary Waters are pit toilets without modern conveniences, including toilet paper, sinks, and most noticeably, walls. The "toilets" consist of a wooden box about two feet high by three feet wide that is outfitted with a seat and lid. They are typically located at the end of a trail, usually about twenty yards from every campsite.

I was pleasantly surprised this trip to find that, over the years, they replaced some of these aging wooden structures with much simpler fiberglass commodes. It doesn't enhance the experience, mind you, but it is nice to know the Forest Service cares enough to replace and improve one of the few essentials your Boundary Waters permit provides.

Timing your bathroom schedule is fairly important when camping in these extreme regions. You don't want to have that late-night nature call if you can avoid it. There is nothing like the feeling of ultimate vulnerability and exposure when you're sitting on a commode in the middle of the woods in the middle of the night, pants around your ankles, waiting for the hungry bear to come ambling through. It's just you, your flashlight, a roll of TP, and your thoughts. Your mind begins to mull things like, "I wonder if this flashlight would hurt a bear if I smacked him on the head?" or "I wonder if anyone's ever been mauled while using this toilet?" These are not happy nature thoughts in bear country at two in the morning.

Another thought that creeps into your head during these late-night bathroom runs is that something might have crawled under the lid before you got there and is awaiting someone to help it out. This causes me to give the toilet lid a good rap before lifting it, just to knock whatever it is back into the deep, unknown recesses before I start my business. It most likely is an unwarranted warning, as I don't know of many toilet-dwelling creatures, but you can never be too sure. Thoughts like these make toileting pretty much a focused affair. It's not like you'd want to bring a magazine with you to these facilities.

The remote location of the outdoor toilet at our site actually caused the kids to memorize the path to it by the landmarks. Always in pairs, they would wander back by the two conjoined trees (the Twin Towers), take a right at the big mossy rock (Plymouth Rock), and then, another five yards or so, go just past the fern patch. They often recited the features as they walked back. When they reached a certain point, one was told to stand with their back turned while the other would continue on to the commode farther into the trees. When one was done, he or she would pass the toilet paper off and switch. Often times, they would talk to each other through the trees just to calm their anxiety about their vulnerability while taking care of business.

The kids always came out gagging and griping about how smelly the thing was. Every trip was the same story. "Ewww, that thing was nasty!" they said, like they'd never been to a pit toilet before. Indeed it was nasty, but it also served as a reminder of all the conveniences we so take for granted back home. This is an especially good lesson for kids of this age. I like to call it *pit-toilet philosophy*. When you're camping, television, video games, and texting are not around. It forces kids not only to amuse themselves but to see that life, when you break it down, really just amounts to eating, sleeping, playing, working hard, and going to the bathroom. Whether you're in the middle of the woods or the middle of the city, it always comes back to the basics. These trips helped bring them back to center and helped them see how good they have it back home, even though they constantly remind us otherwise.

Disaster Averted

Bringing kids to the Boundary Waters was a new undertaking for us. Our trips of twenty years ago were for the adult men of our family. Our wives and girlfriends chose to forgo the inconveniences and unpleasantries of roughing it in the woods. They were completely content to let us go and "get it out of our system" every year while they stayed back and enjoyed their solitude. By bringing up not only kids but girls, we were truly breaking far from the tradition of twenty years prior.

This is not to say our kids had not camped before. We all camped together at state parks a couple of times when they were younger. Those early trips exposed them to all of the fun that comes with a good campout. From a parental perspective, however, much of this time was spent trying to protect them from the dangers of the great outdoors. "Stay away from the fire! Don't play with that axe! Watch out for poison ivy! Put on your life vest!" These are all the standard camping rules parents have been using for years in an attempt to keep their kids from harm's way.

On this trip, because our kids were a bit older and more self-sufficient, there was a tendency to let our guard down a bit and relax. As in everyday life around the house and neighborhood, you occasionally let them stretch their wings as they got older. You turned them loose and hoped some of the common sense you instilled in them would rise to the surface and rule the day. Well, that's how they write it up in the self-help parenting books, anyway.

On the second morning of our trip, while we were getting breakfast prepared, Ben and Hunter wandered off seeking adventure, unbeknownst to the rest of the group. The two, when paired up, could be named "Ding" and "Dong" respectively, as they often found ways to cause trouble when together on vacations. The collective brain trust of these two (and boys this age in general), is small and includes tendencies toward the wildly irrational.

As I was straightening up after breakfast, Hunter ran into camp and said, "Uncle Jim, Ben fell out of a tree and hurt himself!"

"He what?" I asked in disbelief.

"Um, he was climbing a tree and he fell out," Hunter reiterated.

"Where?"

"I can show you. Down by the water." Hunter turned and started walking quickly back down the path.

This is when the adrenaline kicked in. No parent wants to hear their child might be seriously hurt. Thinking the worst, I jumped up and ran quickly behind Hunter as he took me along a narrow path back through the pine trees and ferns. I heard Ben crying as I got closer. As I came to the edge of a small hill leading down to the lake, I saw him lying at the bottom of the hill on a large flat rock, holding his arm. I skittered down the hill to assess his injuries. I asked him what hurt. Tearfully, he said it was his wrist, and it hurt bad. I had him try moving it up and down. I bent it to see if there was any limited movement, protruding bones, or the like. He seemed to be able to move it pretty fluidly, so any thoughts that we might need to splint it and paddle for home were soon quelled.

When he stopped crying and we were assured nothing was broken, I asked him what happened. He said he was climbing a tree and a branch broke off and he fell onto the rock. He pointed to the tree, a dead pine with a set of weathered branches that would tempt any reckless kid. The branches stuck out like telephone pole rungs and presented themselves as an easy climb. Anyone who knows the brittleness of long-dead tree limbs, however, would have seen the potential for disaster right away.

I looked up to the branch that had broken off. It was about six feet off the ground, which meant he'd taken quite a fall. He said the last thing he remembered thinking when he heard the branch snap was, *Uh oh, not good!* He was incredibly lucky to come out of it with a mildly sprained wrist. He could have cracked his head open on the rocks below. Part of me wanted to scream at him and lecture him for his carelessness, yet I was so relieved to see he was okay that I took it easy on him.

"Listen, Ben, the woods are a dangerous place to be doing things like climbing trees. If you had been seriously hurt, how do you think we'd get out of here?" I asked.

As he held his sore wrist in his good hand he answered, "Sorry, Dad. I didn't know the branch would break."

I then reminded him not to wander off and to avoid any dangerous activities like tree climbing, cliff diving, or bear wrestling. Experiences like this teach kids far more than adults are capable of teaching them. A good scare goes a long way sometimes.

The trip reminded us all of just how remote the BWCA is. I remember talking to a coworker long ago about one of my trips and he described how, if someone broke a leg, for example, they would probably have to be strapped down and packed out in anguish. Not at all a scenario I'd wish for anyone and, frankly, one I'd rather not think about. But it is entirely possible. We were only one portage from our vehicle, but in situations where groups traveled four or five portages deep, it could take a couple of days just to get back.

Ultimately Ben's fall served as a teachable moment to the other kids on the trip. It provided lessons like always travel with a buddy or don't climb anything higher than a place from which you would jump. It also reminded me of the responsibility that goes with taking my children into the wilderness. If I drown or maim myself on some man-trip with the brothers, that's my own fault. If my child is injured because I was negligent, I'm not sure I could live with myself. It was a lesson learned and duly noted.

Fishing Economics

A stand-up comedian I once saw made an interesting point about fishing. He said when you added up the cost of the boat, gas, equipment, bait, and man-hours, a pound of fish would cost about a hundred dollars. Now, considering you can get walleye in the store for about eight dollars a pound, it is apparent fishermen are

    A. Not good with numbers

    B. In it for something more than the end product

    C. All of the above

The last day of the 2009 trip proved the comedian's mathematical theorem rather completely. The day started innocently with Sarah, Ben, and me fishing in the morning. Being the last day, we were all determined to get at least one more fish before the trip's end. We paddled slowly across the lake to a bay with a depth we thought might be good for walleye and dropped our rock anchor to the bottom. I grabbed my heavy-action rod and reared back with what I thought was an average cast. On the forward thrust, I heard the telltale plunk of my rod tip splashing into the lake.

"Dang it!" I said.

"What happened, Dad?" Sarah asked.

"My rod tip fell off while I was casting," I replied.

During my retrieval, it became apparent the rod tip had not fallen off but had shattered just above where it joined with the lower half.

"What the . . . ?"

After taking a closer look, it was clear this rod had seen its last cast. If it had happened twenty years earlier, in the midst of a longer trip, I would have jerry-rigged it with duct tape and tried to make it work. Instead, I proclaimed, "Game over for this rod," and put it on the bottom of the boat. Fortunately, I had a second rod and was able to continue fishing. Nevertheless, the broken one added another thirty dollars to the total trip cost. (Ca-ching!)

We managed to catch a few fish that morning, but then things dropped off, so we headed back to camp to fix a shore lunch. Tom prepared the fish we caught using a bit of culinary creativity because we ate all the eggs for breakfast, including the ones we intended to save for fish batter. He improvised by using a bit more butter, water and spices. That is part of the beauty of the Boundary Waters experience. You quickly learned the necessity of rolling with the circumstances and ad-libbing. It's not like you could portage over to the grocery store and pick up some eggs. Improvise, man, improvise! The meal was a hit. My kids, who are normally picky eaters, gobbled it up and still comment today how much they enjoy fish the way Uncle Tom makes it.

With lunch in our stomachs, we packed up the rest of camp and started paddling back toward the short portage that was between us and the boat launch at the outfitters. Thinking this would be a good chance to get some last minute trolling in, I changed our two lines to more appropriate lures. I put a Red Eye spoon on Sarah's line and outfitted mine with a nice big Rapala. Both lures are notorious for attracting walleye and northern pike.

I cast my line directly off the back of the canoe and set my rod behind my seat. I told Sarah to position her rod perpendicular to the boat, off to one side. I paddled at a slow pace toward the portage landing, about twenty minutes away. Rob and Alison gave up any hope of fish at this point and were focusing on forward progress. Tom and Hunter, like us, were determined to fish until the last minute in hopes of dragging something in.

As we approached the shore, I said to Sarah, "Reel it in and get ready to land." As she started to reel in her line, she struggled and then groaned, "Oh, no! Dad, look at this." When I looked, I could hardly believe my eyes. Her line was so incredibly twisted around mine, there was little hope of *ever* untangling it.

Trying to think quickly, I said, "Well, leave it as it is and I'll pull them in manually when we get to shore."

No sooner had I said that than *both* lures snagged on the bottom and stretched our lines taut. Then, *wham-wham!* Both lines snapped cleanly off.

"Well, I guess that solves that issue now, doesn't it?" I said dryly. Sarah laughed at my attempt to make light of the situation. (Ca-ching, ca-ching!)

As I saw it at the time, it was almost like fulfilled prophecy. After all, I hadn't lost any six-dollar lures the entire trip, so it made sense I should lose two in the same instant of the last day. When I assessed the entire situation, it was tempered by the realization that I had just spent three days fishing with my kids in the Boundary Waters. It was worth every cent. If I learned one thing as a kid growing up without a father, it was that you can't put a price on memories.

This one, however, was definitively a twelve-dollar one.

Boys Being Boys

After our portage out of Alton Lake, we began making our way toward the landing on Sawbill Lake. These final minutes of our trip saw the three crews all paddling with different motives. Tom and Hunter fished until the bitter end, still trolling slowly out either side of their canoe, hoping to get one last fish in the boat before landing. Rob and Alison, on the other hand, paddled with intent, looking forward to the second half of the vacation at our timeshare condo on the shores of Lake Superior. The wives and our young daughters were there awaiting our return from the deep woods. We were scheduled to spend two nights at the condo before our return home and, at this point, it was clear Rob was done fishing. This was probably because, overall, the fishing had been a letdown. He was done fishing. Done trying. Done.

Sarah and I paddled our canoe at a leisurely clip, trying to coordinate our strokes to minimize the zigs and the zags. While I wanted to fish, the thought of the work involved in setting up my line again or maybe even losing another lure just sucked out the motivation entirely. My kids were looking forward to the condo and were tired of the woods and water. It was clear they were done, too.

Tom and Hunter eventually gave up their efforts and joined the rest of us in pointing their canoe toward the landing at Sawbill and pushing forward. When we landed, the kids were giddy and squirrelly. There was electricity between them that could not be sequestered or short-circuited. They had been cooped up in a canoe for the last few hours and the price was now to be paid. They were releasing their young energy the only way they knew—through goofy chatter and a lot of good old-fashioned horseplay.

The adults focused on unpacking the canoes and loading the trucks. We shouted orders to the kids in an attempt to get them to pull their weight. They helped a little, but then one or the other got distracted by one of their cousins and started messing around again. Ben, in particular, seemed to be oblivious to any sense of duty or obedience to anything I said to him or anything I asked him to do. I had a couple of tiffs with him on the trip already about doing his share around camp and in the canoes, so his defiance was beginning to grate on me.

"Ben, I said move that stuff from the dock over to the driveway," I nagged.

He met this order with more goofing around with Hunter. The two of them were clearly drunk on each other's presence, with no hope for treatment but an ugly intervention.

Tom and Rob went to get their trucks a short walk from the landing to the outfitters parking lot. I stayed back with the cousins, canoes, and equipment. The kids continued to be kids to the point of annoyance. I was tired after three days of single parenting and, with the realization my BWCA vacation was coming to an end, I was beginning to crack around the edges.

We lifted the canoes onto each truck and roped them on snug for the two-hour trip. I heard Ben getting loud again in Rob's truck and I'd had enough of it. I shouted at him again to stop messing around. He looked straight at me and made some sort of mocking face. Any parent knows the face. The one that screams, "I'm sorry, I was ignoring you. Were you talking to me?"

The gasket blew. I'd had it with his blatant disrespect and I was determined to put it right. If you've ever seen Clint Eastwood's face contort in some of his old Dirty Harry movies, I'm guessing that's how I looked. I'm certain the veins in my forehead were forming peace signs as I gritted my teeth and stomped toward Rob's truck, where Ben was. My heart started to pound as Jekyll Jim turned into Father Hyde. I grabbed his arm tightly and said, "Look here, you little . . . brat, you have done nothing but smart off to me all day. Furthermore, you haven't done your share of any of the work this whole trip." Even though it wasn't entirely true, at the moment it was how I felt. I squeezed his arm tighter as his smug look took flight and he was left with nothing but cold, sober fear.

"Oww, Dad, you're hurting me," he complained as he winced and tried to draw back his arm. My anger gushed like a runaway fire hose. It was his wincing that brought me back to my senses. It ratcheted me down and awakened me to my overreaction. I dropped his arm and left him with a glare. I went back to packing as my blood pressure slowly returned to healthy, chartable levels. Ben and the rest of the kids, sensing my anger, quieted down to a low roar in the truck. When they asked if they could all ride together, Rob elected to take off his hearing aid and take them all in his truck. During the long ride back to the timeshare with Tom, I had a lot of time to think about my outburst. Not only did I call my son a brat in full view of his cousins and my brothers, but I followed it up by hurting the child with my big, meaty hands. Furthermore, this was putting an incredibly sour ending on an otherwise great trip, one I looked forward to for years. I beat myself up pretty good.

Way to go. Way to lose it on the last moment of the last day. What a parting memory to add to the BWCA experience for Ben.

At the same time, none of this is to say the discipline wasn't warranted or completely justifiable. I just wished I had handled it better. Later that evening at the condominium on Lake Superior, I apologized to Ben. I told him that while I was sorry about what I did, he was pushing my buttons and I lost control. He understood and appreciated I took the time to apologize for something so harmless.

People have told me that my dad, at times, had a bit of a short fuse. I have but a handful of memories of him, most of them good and one not so good. I was about four and my family was in a tough financial situation and was living in a housing project in St. Paul. My father had a friend over who was drunk and out of hand. I was playing with a toy car underneath the phone that hung in the kitchen hallway. Dad was fairly ticked off at his friend's condition, so he took it upon himself to call a cab to take the guy home. In his anger to get to the phone, he hurriedly kicked the car out of my hand as he picked up the receiver and started dialing. It's likely he didn't even realize what he did. He was caught up in the moment and was doing whatever he needed to do to fix an unpleasant situation.

I reacted with fear and surprise. I didn't ever remember seeing him exhibit his anger or be this torqued up before. It caught me off guard. Why would a man who never showed anything but love to his kids do something as mean as what he had done?

In my attempt to understand the event, a couple of things have become clear. First, I think this event became ingrained in my mind to show me my dad was human. He had stresses and insecurities unlike any I've ever experienced. He had seven kids to provide for and was probably maxed out most of the time. While the tendency among us children is to make him out to be a hero who died an early death, the fact is, he wasn't perfect. The truth is that my mom is the true hero in our family's story, having picked up the slack of raising all of us after his death. She accomplished the unthinkable and, while my stepfather Jack was also there for much of it, she did the lion's share.

The other thing this incident has shown me is that, as a father, I need to keep my own anger in check. It is indicative of how impacting a single incident can be on a child, even going back decades. I've always said I never really had a temper until I became a father, and now it is something I need to keep an eye on. If these are the only takeaways I get from an otherwise crappy moment growing up, well, they are good lessons learned.

A couple of years later, during the summer of 2011, Ben asked when we were going back up to the Boundary Waters. I was elated to hear him ask the question for a couple of reasons. First and foremost was his interest in returning. It meant the trip in 2009 left a lasting impression on him and he longed to go back. I had done my job and instilled in him an appreciation for the area and the experience. The other reason I was happy was it meant he was over the incident.

It would appear I needed to get over it, too. Losing my temper is nothing any other parent has not done in the heat of the moment. While I hold myself to high standards, I need to understand that it comes with the territory. One might even say it's part of the genetic code of parenting. My dad had done it, I had done it, and Ben probably will too. The important thing is to recognize it, corral it if possible, and if not, at least be man enough to apologize.

Fishing for Answers

The wheelchair-accessible cab pulled into Rob's driveway right on time at two thirty on a Saturday afternoon, Memorial Day weekend of 2011.

"Hey guys, the cab's here," I said to my sister-in-law Jane and my brother Rob as they hustled to finish getting him prepped for the day. When he was ready, Jane rolled him down the homemade ramp that led out of their kitchen into the garage. I loaded our fishing rods and gear into the cargo area while the driver wheeled Rob into the van.

Once the wheelchair was in, the cabbie strapped it in tight, made sure Rob was comfortable, and then put the ramps up and slammed the door. I climbed in the passenger seat in front.

"Have a great time, you guys. Catch a big fish," Jane said through the open window as she turned Rob over to the care of the cabbie with the tobacco-stained grey beard.

"Thanks hon, we will. See you about eight o'clock. Love you," Rob replied, anxious to get on the water.

* * *

Eleven months earlier, Rob had been diagnosed with a chondrosarcoma tumor on his spine. The cancerous growth had been removed in a series of three surgeries in June of 2010. His surgeries were long, difficult procedures conducted by a team of skilled surgeons. Titanium rods, screws, and a wire mesh cage were used to reconstruct his spine in miraculous fashion at the Mayo Clinic. Over the course of the summer and fall, he recovered at home. He returned to work and seemed to be on track for getting back to a routine.

On the day in early December he was to go in for his six-month post-op checkup, he was experiencing numbness in his leg and difficulty urinating. The local doctor recommended he be rushed down to Mayo for emergency surgery to remove a new tumor that was pressing on his spine and causing the numbness. Most of the tumor was removed, but two days later, the oncologist reported the cancer had spread to his lungs. Two difficult rounds of chemotherapy had no effect on the tumors and Rob's condition was deemed terminal. He was paralyzed from the chest down and he would have months, not years, to live.

At Rob's request, a Celebration of Life party was held in his honor in April of 2011. Over four hundred friends and family came to offer support and say their goodbyes. Near the end of the party, the suggestion was made to get the brothers together on a fishing outing one more time before Rob's condition deteriorated. We set the date for Memorial Day weekend and we all hoped and prayed everything would come together.

*　*　*

The cabbie parked the cab van outside Tally's dockside boat rental on White Bear Lake. He got out, opened the back hatch, and freed Rob and his wheelchair from the dizzying web of safety straps and buckles. I wheeled him over to the outdoor deck and we waited for Tom, Paul, and Keith, our "brother from another mother," to arrive. It was then that I heard the familiar beeping of the National Weather Service on the radio inside the boat-rental shack.

"The National Weather Service has issued a tornado warning for Scott and Carver Counties in Southeastern Minnesota. Residents of these areas should take shelter immediately."

The two counties were a fair distance from where we were, but judging from the clouds building to the southwest of us, the possibility of it heading our way wasn't out of the question. I was beginning to wonder if we'd gotten this far only to have our trip thwarted by the weather.

"I just heard there are tornado warnings in Scott and Carver Counties," I told Rob.

"Oh, great!" he said as he looked toward the ominous clouds. Like me, he seemed concerned we might have to call the whole thing off.

Now, I don't often demand anything from God. I know He has a plan and I can respect that. This was different, though. This trip *needed* to happen. This trip *had* to happen. It might be the last time all four of us would get the chance to fish together, and anything short of getting on the water and getting Rob a fish just wouldn't do. I silently prayed a terse little prayer that basically amounted to, "Dear God. Really? C'mon."

Tom, Paul, and Keith arrived and met Rob and me at Tally's at three o'clock. We greeted each other with hugs and handshakes and a quick mention of the radio reports. The boat proprietor said if we saw any lightning, we were to head straight to shore. We promised him we would and rolled Rob down the steep ramp toward the awaiting pontoon. We passed a group just getting off the water who said they had been out for a few hours and hadn't caught a thing. Knowing the collective fishing experience of the Landwehr brothers, I figured we would fare better, but along with the weather news, it was not what I wanted to hear.

With Paul at the wheelchair handles and Tom and I each at a wheel, we lifted Rob onto the pontoon. We positioned him in a spot near the middle of the boat, where there were no bench seats. The cooler and gear were loaded on and we all took our seats, with Tom at the wheel as captain. He fired up the sorely underpowered 25-horsepower Mercury and slowly backed us out from the dock. It was a cool, sixty-two-degree day, but there was no ignoring the foreboding mountain of clouds building behind us as we headed east to our first spot. I set up Rob's rod and handed it to him.

"Thanks, Jim," he said.

"No problem, bro."

We anchored in about seven feet of water and everyone cast their lines. We were all using minnows on jigs underneath a slip bobber, which allowed fishing at a specific depth. Crappies were the goal, but like most of our trips, any kind of action would be welcome. More than anything though, I prayed Rob would catch a fish. This was our day together, but it was really all about him. A fish would be a nice touch.

It began to sprinkle lightly and after a few warning drops, Tom and Paul set up the pontoon's canopy to give us a refuge in case things got dicey. Tornado warnings or not, we were finally fishing! Beers were passed around and an informal can-tinking toast was made.

"Here's to the brothers," Paul said.

"Hear, hear," we answered.

Then the rain came a little harder.

The drops fell slowly at first and steadily increased. Paul and I helped Rob roll his wheelchair under the canopy. We all joined him under it within a couple of minutes, when the rain became downright problematic. With all five of us crammed beneath the undersized canopy, it truly was a Kodak moment. It then occurred to me that here we were again, huddled under a tarp (of sorts) trying to weather a storm like we had a time or two before in the BWCA. It was beginning to look like a lifelong pattern. While we weren't in the Boundary Waters, it was the closest we could hope for given the circumstances, and it sure as heck felt like we were there.

We all started that nervous laughter when it came down hard and steady. "It's always an adventure with us," Rob said.

"Oh, it'll pass. It's just a short cloudburst," Tom added dryly.

I hoped he was right, despite his sarcasm.

After about fifteen minutes, the rain came to an end. I thanked God for the small blessing and helped Rob roll back into his fishing spot. He cast his line out from his chair. The rest of us returned to fishing as well. A couple minutes later, Rob's bobber took a dive. He set the hook and brought in the first catch of the day, a small crappie. We all congratulated him for getting us started.

I guess I can't understate the significance of this fish. Despite the fact it was too small to keep and on any other trip might have driven one or more of us to start ridiculing about its size, this time was different. This one meant that if Rob went the rest of the trip without catching any more, he could say he didn't get skunked. In what might be his last trip fishing with all of his brothers, he'd caught one.

I thanked God for another small blessing.

Rob freed the crappie from his line and we exchanged high fives and fist bumps with him. I began to really appreciate how lucky we were to be together and, frankly, I was relieved Rob landed a fish. His crappie also spurred the rest of us on to try to catch a fish of our own to ensure that everyone got "on the board," as we like to say in the angling world.

Paul handed Rob a new minnow from the bucket and Rob put it on his hook. "Paul, could I get one of those from you too?" I said.

"Sure," Paul said as he reached into the bubbling bucket, fished one out, and handed it to me. The bucket was a high-tech unit I had never seen before. It had a small motorized aerator built into it that kept oxygen flowing to keep the minnows alive. "Hey, that's cool. Does it run on batteries?" I asked no one in particular.

"No, it's solar. What do you think?" Paul said with sodden sarcasm. It was good to know that over the years, none of us had lost a step in the sibling put-down department. Everyone was still fair game and quick to jump at the chance to get a laugh from the others.

Rob was quick to answer with a second fish, this time a small northern pike. I grabbed my camera, switched it over to movie mode, and caught the last few moments of him landing it. He pulled it onto the pontoon's deck and it flipped like, well, a fish out of water. It was at this point I thought, this is outstanding! Here we are trying our best, and Rob was the one catching all the fish, just as it should be. How can this get any better?

After about twenty minutes of no action, we decided to motor over to a small nearby island and try our luck there. Captain Tom fired up the Mercury and we barged on over. On the way, I looked up and spotted an eagle flying overhead. I didn't recall ever seeing a bald eagle that close to an urban area before. They are much more common further north, especially in the Boundary Waters, so this seemed odd. I pointed it out to Rob, who craned his neck to try to see it. He caught the last few moments before it disappeared behind some trees.

As we pulled up to the small island, we noticed a loon's nest with a mother and her chicks. Again, loons this far south and close to the city seemed to be out of place. I hadn't lived in the Twin Cities area for twenty-five years, so maybe they'd been there for a while; I wasn't sure. It brought to mind the crazed loon encounter we had a couple of years before and how grateful I was we had the chance to experience the Boundary Waters together with our kids. In any case, the loon sighting gave me the sense we were much farther north than we actually were. I don't want to say that coming across the loons and the eagle was the hand of God at work, but it sure got me to thinking.

Soon enough, luck picked up for some of the rest of us. Paul and I each caught a largemouth bass, but Rob continued to steal the show. He landed a small perch, one so embarrassingly small he threw it back before we could snap a picture of it. A bit later, he caught a nice largemouth bass. These are notoriously good fighters and this one did not disappoint. It fought valiantly and Rob had fun bringing it in. It appeared at this point Rob was in the zone, and that was okay with those of us who weren't. Today wasn't about us.

After he released the bass, he asked Paul for a new minnow. "Hey, I'll take one too, while you're at it," I said.

"Somehow, I became Bait Boy," Paul said with a hint of disdain. We all laughed at his ability to laugh at himself.

We tried a couple more spots as the afternoon moved toward evening. I checked with Rob to see how he was doing.

"I'm starting to get that kicked-in-the-crotch feeling. I think I'll take one of my pills."He went on to say the doctor told him he could cut the morphine pills in half if he wanted, but Rob didn't see much point in that. It was a barometer of how his condition had deteriorated in the five months since his diagnosis. Rob was beginning to lose weight and strength, and he tired easily. I can't say, given his condition, I didn't agree with the whole-pill mentality. Cancer sucks, and anything that can be done to ease the pain should be done, in my opinion.

The sun hung low in the sky as we enjoyed our waning time together on the big boat. Eventually we approached the hour our boat was due back, so we told Tom to work us back toward Tally's. At this point, Tom and Keith were the only two without a fish. Keith has never been known for his luck, so that was not a big surprise. Tom, on the other hand, was a bit of a shocker. He is not only an excellent fisherman, but he is the commissioner of the Minnesota Department of Natural Resources. He's supposed to be able to will fish into the boat with his knowledge of all things fish and wildlife, and here he was on the edge of being skunked.

Just outside the dock at Tally's, Tom killed the motor and said, "I've had some good success in this area; let's finish out the day here." After a couple of minutes, Rob landed a beautiful bluegill. This was his fifth different species of fish on the day. In addition to this statistic, he finished with the notoriety of having caught the first, the biggest, and the most.

Within minutes of Rob's catch, Tom's bobber took a dive. "Hey, look at this. I got one," he said as he started to reel it in. At that moment, his reel erupted into an incredible rat's nest. The line was snarled around the spool so badly he couldn't even crank the reel. When he realized what was happening, Tom said, "Oh, no! What the . . . ? Oh no!" Determined to not lose the fish, he resorted to the technique every fisherman in the same situation would use: the hand-over-hand retrieve. He pulled the line in as quickly as he could and hoisted a twelve-inch northern pike into the boat.

We all laughed, including Tom. We were glad he hadn't been skunked, after all, but had to laugh at the method by which he broke his dry spell as well as the result. Tom, seeing the irony of the whole thing, took it in stride. He even let me take a picture of him with his snarled reel and his tiny catch of the day. I thought, now there's a picture you'll never see on the front page of the *St. Paul Pioneer Press*.

*　　*　　*

I pushed Rob's wheelchair to the waiting van cab outside Tally's at the seven-thirty pickup time. The same bearded cabbie that dropped us off a few hours earlier wheeled Rob up the ramp and cinched all the safety straps in place. I got in the front passenger seat and we started off for home. As we bumped along Highway 96, I was so moved by the events of the day, I felt compelled to share Rob's story with the cab driver. Rob sat behind us and wasn't able to pick up on what we were talking about. I mentioned his diagnosis in December and how his situation was terminal. I went on and on about how this was likely the last time the four of us brothers would fish together and how much it meant to me. It felt good, almost therapeutic, to tell an outsider what a great day we had.

At the house, the cabbie backed the van up the driveway and partially into Rob's garage. We got out and helped free Rob from the safety tresses and backed his chair down the ramp. As we told Rob's wife, Jane, how things went, the cabbie stood by, listening intently. He was clearly touched by Rob's joy and the fact his cab duties had been a small part of such a significant family event. As Rob paid, tipped, and thanked him, I saw the cabbie's eyes begin to tear up just a bit. He shook Rob's hand with sincerity and said, "You take care now, okay?"

"I will. Thank you again," Rob replied.

Jane rolled Rob up the ramp and into the house as I unloaded the gear from the cab and set it in the garage. I walked in the house as Jane wheeled him into his room. She came out ten minutes later and said that he was already asleep.

Now, I am a very spiritual person. I believe there is a God and He has a plan. The events of that day further solidified my faith in ways inspirational music, stirring Bible verses, or riveting sermons never could. Going into the trip, I had a single heavenly request: let Rob catch a fish. God showed me I think too small. I think mortally small and ask mortally small things of an all-powerful, all-loving

God. He granted my request to the fullest and gave me a day with my brothers I will never, ever forget.

I thanked God for large blessings.

*   *   *

Robert Roy Landwehr passed away on August 30, 2011, after a long, courageous battle with cancer. He was only forty-seven years old. I will always treasure the memories of those trips we took so many years ago. The Boundary Waters is a place where our bonds as brothers were knit together tightly, with permanence and strength. Rob's philosophy that it was a place best experienced with family demonstrated how he valued time spent with them. His spirit of adventure and his love of the Boundary Waters and the great outdoors will live on in his children and family forever.

I miss his smile, his laughter, and his teasing. I miss him *greatly*.

Our Return – 2012

"What do you think about trying to get the kids up to the Boundary Waters next summer?" I asked Tom. It was a warm September evening in 2011. Mom and all of my siblings were sitting around a table on the deck at the cabin in Mercer, Wisconsin, only days after Rob had passed away. We had a family tradition of gathering here at this time of year, and after his death, we all agreed it would provide a chance for us to be together for a few days, to mourn, to remember, and to heal. He loved the cabin and we knew being there would be a fitting way to celebrate his life.

"I like that idea. You know, my buddies and I always go up to Gabbro Lake in the spring and have great fishing. Maybe we could do that with the kids," Tom answered.

"That sounds okay to me. I've been meaning to get them back up there since our trip in 2009. I just think Rob would want us to continue to get his girls up there with the cousins for a few days."

Tom nodded his agreement and the planning was set in motion. It was a bright spot in an emotionally charged weekend. It was good to be around the family and I did my best to maintain my composure. Everyone was hurting but, for the most part, everyone wore their best stoic Scandinavian faces as we came and went between our various cabins. On Saturday night, as I went to hug my sister Jane goodnight, my emotions overwhelmed me and I lost control. "I'm going to miss him so much," I said as burst into tears and buried my face in her shoulder. She grabbed me a little tighter as I sobbed inconsolably in her arms for a minute. The sobs and tears cascaded and rolled, much like they had done for me throughout Rob's illness. The kids, who had been playing a raucous board game a few minutes earlier, gawked at my open display of grief. It was everything a man is taught to never outwardly show, and I did it with abandon.

Then, before I got hopelessly lost in it, I managed to pull myself out. I backed away from the hug and made light of it by saying "Well, now I have a crying headache and I have to go." Jane and the others laughed as I hurried out the door back to the refuge of my cabin, embarrassed to have lost control like I did.

There were several memorable moments in the course of the weekend, but if I had to point to the most healing one, this moment with Jane was it. It was two siblings comforting each other and mourning the death of one of their own. It was an ethereal moment of emotional blood-relative connection and it seemed to fill a hole even God could not, at least not yet. Perhaps He would help later, but at the moment, I needed a human touch. A sister's touch.

* * *

In 2012, the canoeing group was comprised of three adults and four kids. Tom and I made up two of the adults, and my nephew Nick filled the gap left by Rob's passing the prior August. Paul was asked if he could make the trip, but he had work commitments he could not shirk. And so we turned to Nick, the thirty-year-old son of my sister Jane. In some ways, his presence pulled one of the sisters into a trip historically built around the brothers. Nick's father had died suddenly in 2005 at the age of fifty-two, so he was in good company with the rest of the fatherless souls on this trip. In fact, he would pair up in a canoe with Alison in what we joked of as the "orphan canoe." It was this sort of gentle teasing about a raw topic that kept things light and yet real at the same time.

The kids were the same four that came up in 2009: Tom's son, Hunter; Rob's daughter, Alison; and my two kids, Sarah and Ben. Part of my thought in suggesting this trip to Tom was to fulfill a promise to Rob we would continue to take care of his girls. Unfortunately, his youngest daughter, Amanda, was unable to make the trip because of a prior commitment. Tom and I both knew nothing would make Rob happier than to have us bring Alison to a place he held dear to his heart.

And so we set out for the Boundary Waters on a three-night, four-day trip on June 14, 2012. We returned to the area, the beautiful northern wilderness, seeking many things.

First and foremost, we sought the rush of adventure that only places like the BWCA can provide. All of us live comfortable, antiseptic suburban lives most days of the year. The deep wilderness takes away that comfort and replaces it with an appreciation for the quiet, physical beauty of nature. It replaces it with the need for teamwork and selflessness. Most of all, it replaces it with the excitement of what lies around the bend, what lies at the end of your fishing line, and what the weather holds. All of these variables are beyond your control but combine to create the moth-to-flame attraction of outdoor adventure.

We also returned in the interest of strengthening family bonds and continuing the tradition set before us by my father and his siblings. In this case, Tom and I were serving as mentors to the next generation on how to "do the Boundary Waters." After losing Rob in the fall of 2011, we'd all come to realize the brevity of life and the urgency with which we must live it. If you begin to live as if everything you do has lasting significance, even the minutiae take on new meaning. The same was true of vacations and this trip. With a bit of luck, Tom and I would impart to the kids a love and respect for the area and thereby pass the torch. While it's true we went for ourselves, we went even more so for the kids' sake.

And finally, we returned in the interest of doing some serious fishing. In 2009, when we went to Alton Lake, fishing was a bit of a bust, so this time Tom recommended we go to Gabbro. He had considerable success there in the past, and he said the only thing between us and good fishing was a single long portage. I took him at his word, hoping to get some decent fish and perhaps spark the fishing bug in Nick and rekindle it in Alison and my kids. There was no worrying about Hunter; he *always* had the fishing bug.

As in 2009, Tom relayed the meal plans and told me what I needed to bring. He would pick up his share of the meals and I was in charge of mine. This time, much of the food was purchased ahead of time in Milwaukee before I drove up. The kids and I were staying overnight at Jane's house, and after taking inventory, I determined I needed to make a cursory run to the nearby grocery store and pick up a few forgotten items. When I got there, it was strange walking the aisles alone. There was no one to offer advice on whether to get cocoa with or without little marshmallows, no one to laugh with as we joked in the Kool-Aid aisle, and no one to give me that raised-eyebrow look when the register total was flashed.

I sure missed my brother. Lord, how I missed him.

Day 1 – Mayflies

I was fifty yards into the three-quarter-mile portage with a canoe on my shoulders when I started to work up a light sweat. The mosquitoes were voracious, biting any exposed flesh regardless of whether it had bug spray applied. My mind began to question whether I locked the doors to the van after I parked it in the lot at entry point thirty-three on Little Gabbro Lake. In our flurry to get the canoes unloaded and kids set up with packs, I couldn't recall whether I hit the key-fob lock mechanism on my way to the portage trail. My obsession consumed me. What if someone broke into the car and took the GPS and all the cell phones that were locked in the glove box? Or, worse yet, what if they stole the van altogether?

I was unable to let go of the idea, so I lifted the canoe off my shoulders and set it down gently off to the side in the ferns. I ran back up the trail to the parking lot, not wanting Tom and Nick to worry about why I was so far behind them. When I got within range of the van, I hit the key fob to relock what were probably locked doors, anyway. This simple act helped me to sleep better at night, knowing I'd taken all the measures possible to avoid returning to an ugly situation.

I ran back to the abandoned canoe and lifted it onto on my shoulders. It was a lightweight eighteen-foot Kevlar boat rented from an outfitter in Ely. At a meager forty-five pounds, it was twenty pounds lighter and much easier to carry than the Royalex canoes we used in 2009 or the aluminum boats of the '80s. The weight difference scaled a nightmarish portage down to a mere bad dream. I clipped along at a good pace, hoping to minimize my exposure to the heat and bugs.

About a third of the way into the portage, I caught up to Sarah and Alison, who were sitting on the side of the trail, resting and swatting bugs. Because of the number of people in our party and our attempt to make the portage in a single trip, everyone's loads were stuffed to unforgiving weights. The girls' packs were heavy, ungainly, and certainly more than they should have been expected to carry. Seeing them resting this soon was an indicator we overloaded them.

I was sucking wind pretty badly, so I set the canoe down to take a quick break and check on them. "You girls okay?"

"Yes, we're resting. This pack is heavy!" Sarah said as she swatted a mosquito on her arm.

"Yeah, I might have overloaded yours a bit. Tom said this portage was tough, and he wasn't kidding," I replied.

After a minute of catching my breath and swatting my own mosquitoes, I said, "Alright, I'm going to keep going then before these bugs carry me away. See you on the flip side."

I continued down the trail. It was a long, strenuous portage filled with uphill climbs and interspersed with flat, shady stretches that teemed with mosquitoes. My upturned canoe served as a bug coliseum, of sorts, as I walked. They took advantage of my compromised position to suck blood from my hands, wrists, and head. I cursed my shortsightedness in not putting on one of the many head nets we brought that were stuffed away somewhere. Luckily, the last five minutes of the trail finished with a long, forgiving downhill—one I would forget until four days later when the same stretch became a long, unforgiving uphill.

When I got to the portage landing, I hefted the canoe off my shoulders and set it at the water's edge. Nick and the boys were there waiting, their packs strewn about on the flat rocks of the landing. I was never so glad to see a body of water. It not only meant that the tough portage was behind me but that we were on the cusp of adventure. Things got easier ahead.

Eventually Tom and the girls came walking down the trail. Sarah was wearing a different pack and seemed to be less wobbly legged than when I first loaded her.

"Dad, I couldn't get up when I was resting back there. I was like a turtle on its back. A nice guy and his family going the other way came along and asked if I needed help. I said yes, and he grabbed me by the elbows and helped me up. And then Uncle Tom came along and put his canoe down and switched packs with me," she said.

I felt like a schmuck for having left her there, but I had no indication she couldn't get up. My shame was short-lived because she and Alison smiled and laughed as they filled me in on the details. I was relieved she was there with her cousin. I knew it would be good for Alison to be with her cousins over this Father's Day weekend, as well. Together, they could laugh at their plight during incidents like the turtle-pack one. In addition, they were building memories they would never forget, much like their fathers had done years earlier.

I was also a bit amazed at the maturity with which they dealt with the hardship of the portage. I know plenty of teenage girls who would have snapped if they were in the same situation. It seemed that having been through the Boundary Waters experience once before, in 2009, toughened the girls up. With the first funny memory of this trip under our belts, we loaded up the canoes and pushed off into the lake.

* * *

A forty-five-minute paddle later, we arrived at our campsite on a large island. The air over the canoe landing was positively electric with mayflies. Evidently, the weekend we chose was the zenith of their hatch. They're harmless, nonstinging bugs that are more an annoyance than anything. This was of little consolation to the kids, who had never witnessed such a spectacle. They were equal parts freaked-out and curious. When we got out of the canoe, Ben used his paddle like a giant fly swatter, trying unsuccessfully to put a dent in the population.

Once we were over the initial mayfly spectacle, we quickly set up camp as the threat of rain was looming. Tom and I rigged up an overhead tarp, which served us well over the weekend. Within ten minutes of having it set up, the rain came. It was a soft but steady rain and drove us all under the tarp's protection. We watched as the water began to pool in the middle of our vinyl roof. Sarah grabbed the lower half of a nearby fishing rod and propped up the center, pushing the water in all directions off the edges. When she tired, someone else took a shift to keep the water from pooling again.

The only missing piece under the tarp was Rob. It was strange not having him there along with us. In these situations, he always kept an upbeat attitude and his million-dollar smile. I pictured him in his poncho, smiling and saying, "Yep, it's always an adventure in the Boundary Waters!" I missed his humor, his wit, and even his teasing. It may sound strange, but I missed how he appreciated the area. He truly relished the vast, wide-open blue skies powdered with fishbone clouds. He loved fishing and watching the loons on the dead-calm mirrored lakes at sunset. He appreciated the warmth and smell of a campfire at night. Dearest to his heart, though, was the fact he was able to share those moments with his family, both immediate and extended. Rob was nothing if not a sentimentalist. He loved his family.

The rain didn't last and, before long, Tom had dinner underway. On the menu for the night were hot dogs, brats, beans, and mashed potatoes. He prepared it all on the two-burner Coleman stove Mom passed on to him years ago when she downsized from a house to her condominium. Ironically, it was the same stove she cooked dinners on during that trip to Iron Lake in 1976, my first foray to the edge of the BWCA, the trip where it rained and rained and rained. The unit showed its age. It was scratched, stained, and rusted with blotches from grease spatters of thirty years ago. It burned white gas and required pumping and priming, unlike the sleek propane equivalents of today. The flame still burned plenty hot, however. In a strange way, it was comforting to know we could rely on this stove that had been a part of our lives for so many years. It had been through every camping trip we took as a family. It sustained us. I could fully picture Tom's son, Hunter, using it with his cousins on a trip of their own ten years from now. It is an heirloom of a different color.

Occasionally, a wayward mayfly landed near the old stove and Tom flicked the ugly critter away. They continued to be a nuisance through dinner and into the early evening. When they landed on the kids, they twitched and thrashed because of the bug's threatening appearance. The flies had a worm-like body, ridiculously large wings, praying-mantis legs, and long, forked tails that made an ugly bug hideous. Again, they were harmless, but their appearance said otherwise.

After dinner we washed the dishes and got ready for some evening fishing. Our method for dish washing was much more ecologically correct than those trips of the '80s and, because we used the stove to heat the water rather than an open fire, we didn't have to struggle with soot. We followed the guidelines set by the ranger at the station in an attempt to minimize our impact on the area. While I regret some of the eco-mistakes we made when we were young, I was determined not to pass them along to my kids.

With the dishes done, the kids were anxious to wet their lines and see what the lake held in store. We paired up in our canoes and set out along the shoreline to the south of our camp. The evening was cloudy and calm. It wasn't long before Hunter and Tom both had walleye in the boat. Nick was next with his first walleye of the weekend. He was especially excited, as he never considered himself much of a fisherman and had never caught a walleye. True freshwater, sport fishermen consider walleye to be the premier fish — beautiful in color, spunky in fight, and certainly one of the best tasting.

While I was hoping everyone would get a fish, I was rooting extra hard for Alison. Her mother, my sister-in-law Jane, told me prior to the trip that fishing was Alison's passion. It was a love instilled in her by her father and was one pastime she truly got excited about. "She needs to fish with her uncles and cousins, Jim. She loves it," Jane said.

About an hour later, I heard the "Fish on!" call from Nick as Alison fought her catch. When she pulled it over the side, I breathed a sigh of relief. I was glad she was able to get her first fish of the weekend on the first night. It was certain this would be an emotionally difficult weekend for her. Sunday would be her first Father's Day without her dad, and while it helped she was in this place with her uncles and cousins, there were some chasms that just couldn't be filled. Rob would have been proud of this fish and proud of his daughter, and I think, deep down, Alison knew that.

Eventually, Ben landed a walleye of his own. It was clear we were "on the fish" and everybody seemed to be having some luck, including me. The exception was Sarah, who came away with no fish at all. When we paddled back to camp at dusk, I could tell she was upset. I knew the feeling when everyone was getting action except you. I reminded her there was plenty of fishing ahead of us. That was a bit like telling a teenager they have their whole life ahead of them, but it was the only thing I could think of at the time. She was genuinely dejected and I knew nothing would help it but a fish.

Day 2 – Dragonflies

Friday came with clouds and a new bug. After a brief breakfast, we started to get ready for our morning fishing outing when Sarah noticed a few prehistoric-looking bugs crawling on the rocks near the canoes. "Ew, Dad, look at this bug. What is it? What kind of bug is this?" I walked over and took a look. It looked like a cross between a grasshopper, a cockroach, and a cricket. I had trouble identifying it. The only thing I could come up with was that I didn't want to discover its sting inadvertently.

"I don't know, Sarah, I've never seen anything like that. It's probably best to stay away from them, though. You never know."

After a few minutes she came across a carcass-like skin of the same bug. Whatever it was had metamorphosed into something else. As she looked along the shoreline, there were dozens of these things and they appeared to be coming onto land to hatch. Before long, she found one in the process of hatching. It was a dragonfly. Evidently the weekend we chose was not only the mayfly hatch but the dragonfly hatch, as well. We were camped in an entomologic maternity ward, apparently in the ninth month. And to think that I was only worried about mosquitoes! About all we had going for us was the fact that dragonflies feed on mosquitoes. Hopefully they were hatching hungry.

*   *   *

After lunch, most of the kids were fishing from shore. Tom, Nick, and I were cleaning up around camp when I heard Sarah shout, "I think I got one here."

I scrambled through camp and ran down to the shoreline. When I arrived, she was on the tail end of her retrieval. I looked into the water and saw a large northern pike on her line. "Honey, it's a northern! A big one!" I said, feeling as excited as she was. She grabbed the fish around its midsection as I pulled the camera out of my pocket. She stood there tall, beautiful, and proud with her favorite Nebraska Cornhuskers hat on while I snapped a couple of photos. We took the hook out and set it free. Sarah glowed and seemed satisfied and relieved her jinx was finally broken. I rested a little easier, too, knowing both of my kids had big fish to their credit and it was still early in the trip. Having had a taste of the action, she returned to casting the Rapala over and over into the lake. She is more like her dad than she knows.

Sarah's luck was infectious, causing Alison to grab her rod and walk around the bend of the island. She fished there for about a half hour all by herself. She appeared to be isolating and I wondered if she was okay. I tried to guess how she was doing emotionally. She seemed okay around her cousins, but one never knew what memories these times of solitude could dredge up. Fishing may have been her way of working things out, but it's my guess she was doing it because her dad instilled in her a love of doing it.

* * *

Much like the afternoons of twenty years ago, things around camp slowed down between the hours of one and three o'clock. With no electronics to beckon and amuse, the kids were forced to find their own sources of entertainment. Somewhere in the course of the afternoon, Alison came across a baby snapping turtle sunning itself on one of the rocks near the water. It was small enough to easily fit into her hand. She picked it up and brought it to the other cousins and showed it off. They took turns having their picture taken with it. Alison put it right next to her face and Sarah snapped a photo. Sarah put it on top of her hat and Alison took one of her turtle crown. Then it was Ben's turn. They were the turtle paparazzi.

When I saw the creature, it immediately took me back to Keith and his big catch. The baby turtle's pointed nose, clawed toes, and jagged shell were, albeit in microscale, exactly as I remembered on that godforsaken creature from the deep of 1988. It didn't hiss and stink like its predecessor, but it was the object of as much attention, nonetheless. Who knows? It may end up on one of these kids' lines in a few years.

Another afternoon source of amusement was Ben reading snippets to the group from *The Zombie Survival Handbook*. We found it humorous and educational to know that in the event of a zombie uprising, some of the best refuges are prisons and offshore oil rigs. It was also good to know if you choose to hole up in your house, you should only use a bicycle-powered generator, as gas generators attract undue zombie attention. The book was to this generation what the *Star* and *Enquirer* were to my brothers and me on our trips. It was clear that the mindless-reading-material camp legacy had been laid down and heartily embraced by our progeny. I was worried about that.

Friday night around camp was spent telling stories, laughing, and snacking on Jiffy Pop. As Tom shook the Jiffy Pop over the fire, he recounted the product jingle from our era. "Jiffy Pop, Jiffy Pop, the magic treat. It's as much fun to make as it is to eat!" It was a sort of decadent pleasure eating hot popcorn around the fire, and the unconventional cooking method made it just a tad magical. For drinks, the kids drank cocoa or Crystal Light. The adults shared some fine boxed wine—a chardonnay, vintage 2011—that was initially frozen and used as an ice pack, a trick I learned from Tom. The night before, we shared Tom's boxed sangria, so he took delight in teasing me about my choice.

"You brought chardonnay? Do you have any brie and crackers with that?" he chided.

"Hey, I thought it might go better with a fish dinner than a red," I said in my defense.

Despite his joking scorn, he and Nick still imbibed their share before dinner, enjoyed in a weathered plastic cup, no less. We were a cultured lot. Evidently though, sangria is the proper choice in the deep wilderness. I made a note to myself and acknowledged that the teasing spirit of the brothers was alive and well in the far, far suburbs of Ely, Minnesota.

Day 3 – White Mosquitoes from Hell

As discussed the night before, Tom, Nick, Hunter, Ben, and I rose early and went fishing. The girls seemed content to sleep in, though no one thought to ask them. We paddled out to a narrow point near an island that looked promising. Within a few minutes of anchoring, Nick had his first fish, a nice walleye. Over the next two hours, we managed to trade off catching fish, one after another. It was clear we found a hot spot and we took advantage until the bite dropped off.

"We better go in so the girls can fish. They're probably up by now," I said.

"Yep, maybe get some breakfast, too," Nick replied as he reeled in his line.

When we landed at the campsite, the girls and their wrath were waiting.

"Why didn't you guys wake us so we could go fishing?" Sarah asked.

"Yeah, it would have been nice to go fishing with the rest of you. Thanks a lot," Alison chimed in.

It was clear from their posture and demeanor they were angry. The air was tense with estrogenic rage. Even the bugs stopped buzzing, waiting to see what would happen. Nick and I apologized and started building our defensive case—we didn't know, we thought you wanted to sleep in, we figured we'd be back shortly—but the excuses all fell short. We were guilty and we knew it. We earned the flogging we were receiving and we just manned-up and took it. It was a lesson on inclusion we needed to hear so we wouldn't make the same mistake again.

There was one positive outcome of this incident. I considered it a moral victory that both of them wanted to fish badly enough to get angry at being denied the chance. It seemed this trip really infected everyone with the fishing bug and this was evidence. Each of the kids showed it in different ways. I knew Sarah was hooked when she cast out her line to troll whenever we moved from spot to spot. As the weekend progressed, Nick's focus around camp was to get the meals out of the way so we could get back to fishing that much sooner. Ben specifically asked us to wake him that morning, so I knew he was another convert. On this trip, Tom and I were planting and watering the seeds for the next generation to appreciate fishing and the bonds that come along with it.

It seemed they were starting to take root.

* * *

After breakfast, I wanted to make up for my transgression by giving Sarah the chance to get some fish. Everyone else was stoked to get more fishing in as well, so the entire party loaded up the canoes and we pushed out onto the water. It was cloudy and there was a decent breeze as Sarah and I pushed hard out to a humpback rock about a ten-minute paddle away. We had success by it the night before, so thought we would try it out again.

We arrived and I dropped anchor. After a few minutes, the wind pushed us perilously close to the rocks. Our anchor was not holding us against the wind's buffeting force, and it seemed every time I adjusted the canoe to a better position, we were blown off course. We spent more time adjusting and correcting than we did fishing.

"This isn't working out, Sarah. Let's try the back side of our island so we can get out of this wind," I said.

I pulled up anchor and we started toward the island. It was only a five-hundred-yard stretch between us and the island, but it was deep water in the middle of the lake. We paddled hard against a relentless, annoying crosswind. From the stern, I tried to power the canoe directly into it in an attempt to tack or "beat into windward," as the nautical phrase goes. For every few strokes of correction, however, we suffered a stiff gust that took the bow and pushed us back off course.

"Paddle hard, Sarah, this wind is kicking our butts."

"I am, Dad. I thought we wanted to go over there though," Sarah said as she paused and pointed toward the island with her paddle.

"Don't stop paddling, Sarah! We do want to go over there, but we're fighting a losing battle here," I said curtly. Her momentary paddling break allowed the wind to again take control of the canoe and push our bow away from our intended destination. Despite attempts to go forward, we were slowly losing ground and being blown across the lake.

I didn't want to clue Sarah in that I was getting concerned. We were up against a strong wind and I was beginning to tire. She was doing her best, but even with a strong paddler in the bow, we would still be struggling. When it became clear we couldn't maintain a direct line to the island, I had to dial up an alternative plan. Because the winds are almost always less intense near shore, I decided we should head toward the nearest shoreline. It would add some distance and time to get to our island location, but it would significantly lower our chances of swamping in the middle of the lake, every canoeist's nightmare.

After a ten-minute push, we neared the shore and, as I'd hoped, the situation was much more manageable. "Now this is more like it," I said.

"Yeah, that was no fun. This is better."

We worked our way up the shoreline, crossed a shallower channel, and made it to the back side of our island. As we paddled up the shoreline of the island, Sarah trolled out the front. Before long, she had a fish on her line. I maneuvered the boat into position so she could land it and she pulled in a nice eighteen-inch walleye. Her spirits lifted immediately. Within forty-five minutes, she caught two more and I managed to catch a couple myself. We found our own little hot spot.

It was a moment I'd like to suspend in time forever. If I could, I'd bottle it, shrink wrap it, and freeze-dry it. Here I was fishing with my daughter in one of the most pristine natural areas of the country. I'm certain she was not aware of the emotions I experienced as she sat in the front of the canoe, fishing her heart out. While we talked about high school life, family issues, and past vacations, I couldn't help but appreciate her smiling in her slightly dirty red shirt, life vest, and jeans. All the while, she was trying to hide a bad case of "camping hair" underneath her backwards Cornhuskers hat. It wasn't necessary because then and there, she was the most beautiful girl in my world.

*　　*　　*

Later that day, we flagged down the other two canoes and we all hooked up in the water. After fishing together for a short time, the skies started to look ominous. We pushed on home and just after we pulled the canoes up to the shore, the rain started. The thunderclaps we heard previously sounded distant and nonthreatening but, true to our fears, the storm came our way. The kids ran to the nearest trees to stay dry while Tom, Nick, and I began putting exposed equipment underneath the suspended tarp. I dug the ponchos for the kids out of the equipment pack and put my vinyl rainsuit on. When it appeared the rain was going to continue for a while, the kids retreated to a tent. I didn't realize until a little later that the tent they chose was mine.

Lightning began to flash and, despite the relative security of our open-air kitchen under the tarp, Tom, Nick, and I questioned the wisdom of seeking shelter under it when it was tied to, among other things, one very tall tree. We took the lightning as a sign and headed to our tents while the storm was at its peak. I scrambled over to the one Ben and I had been sharing all weekend and found that all four teenagers were in it. There was giggling and tomfoolery seeping from all corners. Whenever thunder cracked, one or another of the kids jokingly screamed, which set the other three into more uncontrolled tittering. I smiled at their ability to make the best of a crappy situation. It was clear the rain bothered me more than them, and I was okay with that.

I ran back to the equipment pack and grabbed a stack of card games I brought for situations just like this. I returned to their tent, unzipped the flap, stuffed the games inside, and said, "Here's some games, guys."

"Thanks, Dad," Sarah replied.

By default, I was relegated to the girls' tent next to my own. Their tent was small, short, and uninviting. It was more like a two-person fabric coffin. Barely passable for two teenage girls, it was in no way designed for a person of my height of 6'5". I needed to escape the rain and bugs, though, so I climbed in, rain gear and all. I spent the next ten minutes trying to extricate myself from my hiking boots and vinyl rain gear without kicking or punching a hole in the godforsaken hobbit shelter. Removing the wet raincoat in such a small space was like trying to free myself from a straitjacket while in the trunk of a compact car. Tendons and muscles were stretched to new limits. A shoulder dislocation and a rotator-cuff tear later, I was able to wriggle free from my vinyl coat.

I rested for thirty seconds and plotted my strategy for the rain-pant removal, which, it appeared, would prove equally as tricky. After I removed my boots, I lay on my back, kicked my legs against the hobbit ceiling and wriggled like a caterpillar in metamorphosis. The pants resisted at every joint—hip, knee, and ankle. From outside, it probably looked like an assault was taking place in the tent, and, in some ways, it was. At least it felt like one had by the time I wrestled the rain pants off.

Now that I was marginally more comfortable in my nylon tomb, I decided to try to get a bit of rest. Camping is work, without question, so I saw this time during the rain as a good chance to recharge a bit before dinner. I lay down and stretched out as much as I could. I shut my eyes and listened to the kids playing Uno in the tent next to me. It sounded frenetically out of place in the quiet wilderness, especially given the hard rain. At the same time, it sounded beautiful and familiar. It did my heart good to know the kids were having so much fun in a place that meant so much to me. It brought back in vivid detail the memories of the rainstorms at Iron Lake, of Santana's "Evil Ways," and of cribbage in the tent with my stepbrother, Timmy. I secretly wished this memory would stay with them as well as mine had.

*   *   *

After dinner that night, we were all fishing near the same humpback rock formation Sarah and I tried earlier in the day. The rain stopped shortly after dinner and we were graced with a calm, cool evening. The fishing was fair with a walleye here and there over the course of an hour or so. Before long, we started noticing some annoying insects beginning to appear. They were white and had the buzz of a mosquito and the wings of a small moth. We didn't have our head nets in the canoes, so we had to put up with them landing on us and buzzing near our ears. They didn't bite and, at first, they were just a minor inconvenience. As dusk approached, they seemed to be massing and conducting some sort of uprising or "gathering at the rock." The buzzing was the worst part, triggering our mosquito-slap instincts.

"What are these things anyway?" Alison asked.

"I'm not sure," I answered.

Nick chimed in with, "I think they're white mosquitoes from hell. They're everywhere and they're starting to bug me. What do you think, should we get out of here?"

"I think so. I came out here to get *away* from bugs," I replied.

We quickly pulled up our anchors and moved on to a bug-free zone. There seemed to be a pattern where we were exposed to a new bug every day on this trip. I talked to some people later who told me they were probably just white mayflies. I'm no entomologist, but I thought Nick's description was much more befitting.

Day 4 – Mosquitoes

The next morning, Sarah and Alison elected to sleep in while the rest of us woke early for one last attempt at fishing. At this point in the trip, the girls had had enough mosquito swatting and fishing and were ready to get back to civilization. The five of us males had decent luck for a couple of hours before the bite diminished.

There was one tragicomedy during the outing. Tom was trying to tie Hunter's biggest walleye of the weekend onto the anchor rope because all the clips on his stringer were full. I was watching his valiant efforts when suddenly the fish flipped out of his hand and splashed into the lake. Tom looked over at me with raised eyebrows and a grin and put his finger to his lips. I laughed and nodded.

About a half hour later I heard Hunter say, "Dad, let me see my big walleye again."

Tom started his song-and-dance routine with, "Uh, Hunter, I've been meaning to tell you some bad news . . . "

Hunter took the news about as badly as expected. He loves fishing, and to take away his prize fish of the weekend before he could get a picture with it or show it to his cousins was a kick in the teeth. It was an honest mistake and one Tom and I will likely laugh about for years to come. It's also one Hunter will probably never forget, but he won't be laughing about it.

We paddled back to camp about ten thirty and began to pack up. The kids were feeling the effects of four days without a shower and focused their efforts to speed the packing. They helped where they could and stayed out of the way where they couldn't. Again, their maturity level was markedly different from the trip of 2009, and it made it easier for those of us who were getting to the age where a little help is welcome.

When we finished, we formed up by the canoes for some pictures with the fish. Sarah set up the point-and-shoot camera on a rock and set the mode to self-timer. She pressed the button, raced back to the group, and grabbed the end of the fish stringer next to Alison. It was a classic photo with everyone smiling and the lake, the sky, and the white bloated clouds of northern Minnesota in the background. It was one for the albums, for sure.

There was one more task that needed to be accomplished before we left. I reached into my pocket and pulled out the small Ziploc bag with "Rob's Ashes" written on it in marker.

"Okay everybody, we're going to sprinkle Rob's ashes now. Alison has requested that everyone sprinkle a little portion, but I think it's only right, with today being Father's Day, that she go first," I said to the group.

Alison came over and held out her hand as I grabbed a handful of the coarse, white ashes and put them into it. Alison stepped out onto what we jokingly called "contemplation rock," paused for a minute, and then tossed the ashes over the water. No one spoke. This was a moment between father and daughter, as the holiday was meant to be. I cannot begin to fathom what emotions were going through her at the time, but she faced them with strength and courage.

I continued on in the same way to the next person, and the next. Not much was said during these moments. Everyone spread his ashes over the water except for Tom, who sprinkled his portion around a nearby tree, saying Rob would like a good place to camp. The kids were reverent and respectful the whole time. It was clear they understood the event's significance to Alison as well as them. In a weekend jammed with adolescent craziness and the rattle and hum of teenage energy, the mood at the moment was nothing short of spiritual.

With the last portion of the ashes left for me, I walked over to "contemplation rock." I climbed out onto it, grabbed the baggie by the bottom seam, threw the ashes to the wind and said, "Love ya, bro!" The ashes rained out over the water, leaving a long, linear translucent sheen on the surface. No one spoke for probably ten seconds. It seemed an eternity. We were all caught up in the magnitude of the moment and were collectively speechless. It was moving and powerful. We, seven people Rob held dear to his heart, were spending time together and making memories in a place very special to him—the Boundary Waters. This trip was not a goodbye but rather a reminder that we will return . . . and he will be right there with us.

*   *   *

We pulled into the portage and climbed out of the canoes. These rocky landings near the water were a welcome respite from the bugs. We all knew what the hot portage trail ahead held in store. It would be a buggy mess. Everyone put on their head nets. One of the sanity-saving items of this trip for me was Rob's old mosquito jacket. It was a hooded long-sleeved jacket that covered your entire upper body except your hands. I pulled it out of my pack and put it on. We were going into a combat zone and we needed to be prepared.

I told Nick I would take the first shift with one of the packs as well as the canoe. The long uphill climb I faced would be difficult, but like the rest of my party, I was beginning to taste the nearness of home and the creature comforts that come with it. That would be enough to motivate me to make a run of it.

Nick helped me load the backpack and then the canoe after that. I set off with my ungainly load as Nick trailed immediately behind me and offered encouragement. The climb seemed to go on forever. The humidity of the shady forest hung heavy. The buzz of the occasional mosquito trying to penetrate my hood net motivated me to push harder. It wasn't long before I was breathing hard and deep. As much as my mind tried to focus on one step at a time, it kept switching channels to the one playing reruns of pain, fatigue, and breathlessness.

About halfway up the portage, I told Nick I needed to take a break. I don't like giving up, but at fifty-one, I was a much better manager of my pride than I used to be. I was gassed and sucking all the available oxygen out of the forest. My respiratory needs were actually suffocating other animals, or so it seemed. I set the canoe down and Nick helped me get my pack off. We both had a good laugh at my condition.

"That kinda sucked, eh? You want me to take the canoe for the next stretch?" Nick offered.

"Yes it did and, yeah, that would be great," I said. "I can get the pack."

We both took another couple of minutes to rest and then Nick loaded the canoe on his shoulders and started down the path. Within ten minutes, we were at the parking lot. Tom and the rest of the kids were there waiting. I gave Sarah the keys to the van and told her to bring it around so we could start loading the gear and canoes. Immediately, Ben and the cousins asked if they could go with her. There's evidently big appeal for teens in watching a newly licensed peer drive a vehicle fifty yards on a gravel road. The kids walked off tittering and laughing.

Sarah pulled the van around and parked it on the shoulder. As Tom, Nick, and I prepped the canoes and put the racks on the vehicles, the kids horsed around in the van. Thankfully, the noise level was deadened by the windows, which were closed to keep out the mosquitoes. The kids were busy laughing, screaming, and taking pictures with their phones. Obviously, the sadness of a few hours earlier was taking a back seat to the joy of now, the joy of cousins, and the joy of family. They were over the bug bites, the heavy packs, and the bad weather and had returned to their regular programming.

Watching them giggle, goof around, and recount the stories of the previous few days reminded me of the giddiness my brothers and I shared at the end of our trips so long ago. Every year culminated in the realization we were creating a tradition by leaving the world behind and relying on each other to tighten up our relationship. The trips helped us to understand the importance of family, as messed up and unkempt as it sometimes is. Through these shared adventures, we forged bonds that stood the test of time.

Now, here were our kids creating their own past. I wondered if their memories of the BWCA would have the same impact on them as they had on me. Would these adventures with their cousins knit them together like they had for us brothers? I can't be sure. From what I saw on this trip I do know they are a resilient, tough bunch, full of love for each other. Those qualities will carry them far in life, and it's my hope they will one day carry them back to this special place called the Boundary Waters.

Epilogue

An e-mail from my sister Jane, dated June 23, 2012 (Parentheses mine):

Tonight I had the privilege of sitting down to a birthday celebration dinner with the most cherished people in my life. Nick, Stephanie, Jennifer (daughters), and I gathered together to celebrate the birthday of the newest member of our family, Janet (Nick's fiancée). The conversation led to Nick's recent trip to the Boundary Waters. I was so sure that he would share his story of hell. Much to the absolute surprise of all of us, Nick entertained us with the most inspirational stories. We listened to him, with no exaggeration, for at least an hour. He shared with us the most amazing stories. And these stories, while they had your typical fish stories, were more than that. His true and heartfelt stories were more than you can ever imagine. With the most sincere and total gratitude, Nick relayed to us an experience of a lifetime. One of which I truly wish I could someday experience. Jim, if only you could have heard him. Complete and total contentment. He was a person who I believe had a life-changing experience. He couldn't get it out fast enough. His enthusiasm, and the genuine and heartfelt stories of the trip, was something we all sat and listened to in awe. He spoke so highly, and with so much admiration, of the men that you and Tom are. My heart was truly full. At that moment I cannot tell you whom I was more proud of. The man that my boy has become, to be able to recognize the love of the family, a family that he was so fortunate to be born into, or of the men that just made him realize what it is to be a man of character and integrity. That those men are all my family just overwhelmed me. How fortunate am I to have them all in my life. I thank you. I thank you for who you are. I thank you for embracing my son in the way that you have. He had an amazing father. He loves him unconditionally. I thank God that he has his amazing uncles to continue to hold him closely and give him the love that one would think only a father could. Thank you for that. He was raised to respect. He has the utmost respect for his uncles. I wasn't there, but he realized during this most amazing trip that his respect was tenfold. His admiration for his uncles is beyond words. Thank you, my brother, for being the most amazing and inspirational man I am blessed to know. I always knew you and Nick had a special bond. What happened in the Boundary Waters was Godsent. You are one exceptional man. And I am proud to call you brother. And more than that, I LOVE being your sister. I hope I can pay this back in my love for your kids. Someday I hope you really get this. It is awesome. – Jane

THE END

About the Author

Jim Landwehr enjoys writing creative non-fiction, fiction, and poetry. He has non-fiction stories published in *Boundary Waters Journal, Forge Journal* and *MidWest Outdoors Magazine.* His poetry has been featured in *Verse Wisconsin, Torrid Literature Journal, Echoes Poetry Journal, Wisconsin People and Ideas Magazine,* the *Wisconsin Poets Calendar, Off the Coast Poetry Journal, Heavy Bear,* and many others. He also has a fiction story published on the *Free Zombie Fiction Blog.* Jim lives and works in Waukesha, Wisconsin with his wife Donna and his two children, Sarah and Benjamin.

CPSIA information can be obtained at www.ICGtesting.com
Printed in the USA
LVOW05s2133231014

410305LV00011B/230/P

9 781632 130280